Creating the Ultimate Lean Office

Creating the Ultimate Lean Office

A Zero-Waste Environment with Process Automation

Raymond S. Louis

New York

Most Productivity Press books are available at quantity discounts when purchased in bulk. For more information, contact our Customer Service Department (888-319-5852). Address all other inquiries to:

Productivity Press
444 Park Avenue South, 7th Floor
New York, NY 10016
United States of America
Telephone: 212-686-5900
Fax: 212-686-5411
E-mail: info@productivitypress.com
ProductivityPress.com

Library of Congress Cataloging-in-Publication Data

Louis, Raymond S.

Creating the ultimate lean office : a zero-waste environment with process automation / By Raymond S. Louis.
p. cm.
Includes index.
ISBN 978-1-56327-371-1 (alk. paper)
1. Office management–Automation. 2. Office practice—Automation. 3. Industrial efficiency. I. Title.
HF5548.L68 2007
651.8—dc22

2007034844

11 10 09 08 07 5 4 3 2 1

CONTENTS

ACKNOWLEDGMENTS

To my wife, Laurie: Thank you, for your patience and understanding as I write yet another book.

Thanks also to my colleagues Scott Myers, Charles Louis, and Brett Card, who reviewed key portions of the text and offered insights and recommendations, and whose valuable input was appreciated. Many thanks as well to Paul McGrath who inspired my interest in creating a workshop based upon my implementations and who has been a valuable source of information on many occasions. I am also grateful to Maura May and Michael Sinocchi of Productivity Press, who accepted this work, and to Tere Stouffer, freelance project editor, who developed the book's content, copyedited the text, and enhanced its presentation.

INTRODUCTION

Competition today is global, intense, and continues to escalate as the number of entrants worldwide increases. The application of lean manufacturing techniques are no longer confined to the few organizations that "discovered" and adopted lean in its early years but is being applied globally. In fact, lean manufacturing is no longer a guarantee of competitive advantage; it has become a prerequisite for staying in business.

The principal reason lean manufacturing is being adopted worldwide is that it is effective. Lean manufacturing clearly defines waste, which provides the ability to recognize it, and is complemented by the specific lean manufacturing techniques that are designed to eliminate it on the shop floor.

But there is more to a manufacturing organization than manufacturing. Another significant cost component resides in the office. In fact, in many organizations, administration costs are many times higher than manufacturing costs and there is intense pressure to reduce it. Service organizations, such as hospitals, insurance companies, and banks, are also under extreme pressure to reduce their administration costs because it is an extremely large component of total costs. The overall estimate of administration costs in relationship to total costs ranges from 25 percent to 60 percent, depending on the type of industry.

In connection with this, it has become apparent to a number of lean practitioners over the past few years that lean manufacturing techniques also offer opportunities to reduce administration costs in the office. The first challenge encountered with this approach, however, is that the manufacturing definition of waste must be changed to embrace the office environment so as to provide waste recognition. The second challenge is that most lean manufacturing techniques are not directly applicable to the office. Examples can stem from trying to linearize work flow (for example, load smooth) when, in fact, forces external to the company control the timing and volume of work that is thrust upon the office.

An example is receiving requests for quotes (RFQs) from numerous potential customers. In a manufacturing environment, various techniques can be employed to meet customer demand within customer expectation during peak periods (such as carrying finished goods in inventory), thus creating and maintaining a linear build within the factory. This type of solution is not possible in most offices which, as an example, cannot have premade unique request for quotes responses readily available sitting on the shelf!

There are, however, some aspects of lean manufacturing techniques that are noteworthy in their application to the office, such as some form of process mapping, asking the five whys to determine root cause issues, and the application of visual factory. But beyond gaining visibility of the current process, discovering root cause issues, and organizing the office, waste elimination in most cases will not occur to significant levels in the office simply by applying lean manufacturing techniques.

Another popular approach in trying to reduce administration cost is the use of off-the-shelf software solution(s). The issue is that standard off-the-shelf software is designed to operate in a multitude of environments. Often, the techniques applied by the software are not compatible to your specific environment, rendering the software less usable and/or forcing the user to perform a plethora of non-value-added activities to make the software function properly. In addition, the conforming aspect of the software package in regard to adopting specific processes often eliminates the competitive differentiation that a company may have once enjoyed. Finally, the techniques employed by the software are typically not innovative; some, in fact, can be several years old by the time the software becomes available.

The answer to leaning out the office begins with a new definition of waste, backed by a set of techniques designed to eliminate waste and streamline non-value-added activities. The definition of waste in the office goes one step further than the lean manufacturing definition because any office activity that adds value or is necessary to perpetuate the business (that is, *required activities*) is considered waste if it can cost-effectively be automated by the computer and is currently being manually performed. The technique employed to eliminate this waste of manually performing required activities is referred to as *administration automation*. It permits users to design processes to meet the needs of their environments, which are then automated without, in the majority of cases, changing source code.

The inherent advantage of being able to customize and automate processes over any other technique is that, 1) a multiplier effect occurs as the people are freed from performing mundane required activities to performing strategic-level activities, and 2) it enables the creation of innovative solutions and services that are typically beyond the scope and capability of the competition. There is almost nothing worse than spending thousands upon thousands of dollars on computer systems only to become another "me too" company whose software solution is not appropriate for the environment in which it is placed.

Creating the Ultimate Lean Office is the product of twenty years of experience. I have applied the techniques described in these pages to create office environments (most recently in a mortgage banking company) that enjoy a competitive advantage far better than any which can be achieved by a reliance on commercial, off-the-shelf software. The book clearly defines office waste and demonstrates how to create processes consisting of only required activities and automate those processes to create a multiplier effect. Each chapter provides an easy-to-use, step-by-step process of eliminating waste and streamlining non-value-added activities in the office. The sixteen chapters are grouped into three parts:

Part 1: Achieving a Lean Office through Administration Automation introduces the challenges of attempting to apply current methodologies to create a lean office. It then provides the foundation and framework necessary to understand lean office tools that can eliminate waste and elevate the administration office from simply performing tasks to performing strategic-level activities.

- **Chapter 1—The Lean Office:** This chapter discusses the typical problems that are prevalent in today's administration processes and explains the two most popular approaches currently used to create a lean office environment.
- **Chapter 2—Administration Automation:** This chapter provides a definition of waste as it pertains to the office and reflects on thirteen common forms of office waste. Additional definitions that form the foundation for understanding administration automation methodologies and its objectives are also provided, along with a chart for rating your own status and progress in creating a lean office.
- **Chapter 3—Automating Administration Processes:** This chapter introduces the seven steps of administration automation, which is a top-down approach in aligning the processes to meet the strategic needs of the company, and provides the methodology for creating a lean office. The chapter also contains examples of tasks that are typically automated and gives two examples of a full lean office conversion.

Part 2: System Enhancement Options describes in detail the system enhancement options that you can employ in automating the newly created lean processes developed by the business process improvement team.

- **Chapter 4—The Bolt-On System Enhancement Option:** This chapter explains the typical issues associated with employing bolt-ons and the appropriate steps in making the proper selection, where applicable.
- **Chapter 5—The Extension System Enhancement Option:** This methodology can be employed if source code is available or if an existing program has a "hook." The chapter explains how a copy of the existing module can be made—and then modified—according to the design of the business process improvement team. The original module is left untouched. This chapter also explains how designers of systems often put "hooks" into place in their modules, permitting users to add additional functionality to current software. Design forms and examples are provided.
- **Chapter 6—The Supplier Modification Enhancement Option:** This chapter guides the business process improvement team in determining the gaps between what is required and what is available in the programs offered by suppliers. It also explains how to communicate the desired modifications to suppliers.
- **Chapter 7—The Custom Routine System Enhancement Option:** This chapter is devoted to custom routines, which comprise a highly flexible and powerful mainstay of administration automation enhancements. The scope of application can range from automating simplistic tasks to creating a fully automated supply chain system

without (in most cases) changing source code. The chapter provides the basic guidelines on how to apply this system enhancement option.

- **Chapter 8—The System Enhancement Selection Process:** Often, more than one system enhancement option can be applied to gain the required automated capabilities. This chapter offers guidance on the key factors that should be considered during the selection process.

Part Three: Seven Steps of Administration Automation explains in detail each of the seven steps necessary for creating a lean office and includes illustrative examples.

- **Chapter 9—Step 1: Improvement Driven by Strategic Objectives:** This chapter explains how external and internal analysis is used to determine the strategic objectives of the company and why it is used to guide the lean office conversion.
- **Chapter 10—Step 2: Selecting the Team and Putting Primary Measurements in Place:** This chapter discusses the process of selecting the team leader and team. It also explains the importance of primary measurements used in gauging the effectiveness of the newly implemented processes.
- **Chapter 11—Step 3: Determining Root Cause Issue(s) and Understanding Affected Process(es):** This chapter covers the methodology of determining the root cause issue(s) and the associated affected processes.
- **Chapter 12—Eight Key Questions:** Once the root cause issue(s) and affected process(es) are identified, a standard set of questions validate that administration automation is the appropriate solution. This chapter covers these questions and the rationale behind them.
- **Chapter 13—Step 4: Developing the Solution:** This chapter describes and illustrates an innovative team process improvement chart that can be used by the business process improvement team to design new processes, which are then placed on a future process sequence chart that facilitates system enhancement option(s) consideration and selection.
- **Chapter 14—Step 5: Preparing for Implementation:** This chapter discusses the importance of an implementation milestone chart and how to construct it. It also explains the need for performing cost-benefit analysis.
- **Chapter 15—Step 6: Approval and Secondary Measurements:** This chapter covers two presentation packets used to obtain executive level approval. A primary packet summarizes the project, and a secondary packet contains the details. The importance of secondary measurements is also discussed.
- **Chapter 16—Step 7: Implementation:** This chapter discusses the process of implementation. It addresses the areas that require attention during and after implementation to ensure that all goes as planned.

Keep in mind that a book can go only so far in imparting knowledge; for knowledge to be useful, it must be understood in the context of the environment in which it will be put to use. Also keep in mind that an Information Technology (IT) programmer, someone who has intimate knowledge of the computer system that is in place, must be on your business process improvement team. Prior to implementing any computer enhancements (purchased or programmed in-house), IT needs to ensure that those enhancements will not adversely affect any other part of the system. This book, in the hands of a business process improvement team applying due diligence, can create a lean office that can compete vigorously against the best in the world.

PART ONE

Achieving a Lean Office through Administration Automation

One of the greatest costs for most manufacturing and service entities is administration. It is estimated that administration costs, depending on the type of industry, can be as high as 25 percent to 60 percent of total cost. This means that a significant opportunity to reduce administration costs through the elimination of waste and reduction of non-value-added activities exists, as does the potential to create a rapid, accurate, and cost-effective means of delivering superior value to the customer and thus, effectively perpetuate the business.

In most cases, cost savings can be accomplished by employing the seven steps of administration automation, which can identify and eliminate waste and reduce non-value-added activities, thus redirecting attention to *required activities*. These required activities consist of 1) value-added activities that create value for the customer and 2) essential non-value-added activities that are required to run the business. These required activities are then computer automated to the fullest extent possible, creating a multiplier effect that elevates the office staff from people who perform repetitious manual tasks to people who perform strategic-level activities. The seven steps of administration automation are applied when competitive innovations are sought or when a company needs to dramatically improve speed, accuracy, costs, or timeliness of completion.

To begin the process of creating a lean office, you must 1) understand the strengths and weaknesses of lean manufacturing techniques and commercial off-the-shelf software; 2) learn the foundation and framework of lean office, including the thirteen wastes found in the office; and 3) master the seven steps of administration automation. This material is presented in the following three chapters.

The Lean Office

1

Lean manufacturing uses some well-known definitions of waste, non-value-added activities, and value-added activities, all of which make targets for improvement visible:

- Taiichi Ohno viewed waste (as it pertained to work) as, "The needless, repetitious movement that must be eliminated immediately" (Taiichi Ohno, *Toyota Production System*, Productivity Press, 1988). Simply put, waste is any activity that adds costs but does not add value to a product. This activity is not required at all and should be eliminated. Toyota has identified seven types of waste: overproduction, wait time, transportation, overprocessing, inventory, motion, and defects. These wasteful activities should be eliminated.
- *Non-value-added activities* are considered waste because they do not add value for the customer but are required under the present working conditions. Examples include machine setup and daily work area cleanup. The objective with lean is to reduce these activities, if not eliminate them.
- *Value-added activities* are any activities that change the shape or configuration of a product in a way that creates value for the customer.

The lean office, like lean manufacturing, consists of extremely powerful tools used in making dramatic leaps in improvement and adheres to similar (if not entirely identical) principles. Prior to applying these lean office tools however, the key characteristics of an ineffective administration process must be understood.

Ineffective Administration Processes

Ineffective administrative processes typically have the following characteristics:

- **Disjointed:** The process transcends departmental boundaries. Concentration for each department is focused on its individual tasks, versus having one person responsible for accomplishing the overall process. This fragmentation creates delays and communication issues, both internally and externally (for example, a customer calls in for status and is connected to a number of different departments in an attempt to obtain this information).

- **Loaded with waste:** In many organizations, the administration area is seldom (if ever) thoroughly reviewed from a waste-elimination standpoint. (Recall that the definition of waste is the needless, repetitious movement that must be eliminated immediately.) There are countless examples of what constitutes waste in the office, and one all too common waste is placing the same item on order with the same supplier time and again.
- **Loaded with non-value-added activities:** In many companies, the administration area is seldom thoroughly reviewed in light of its improvement potential—that is, for something that might minimize non-value-added activities. Non-value-added activities do not add value to the customer and must be viewed as waste; paradoxically, some of these activities are essential to business operations and must therefore be seen as "required activities." Since the objective of the lean office is to perform only required activities, which include value-added activities and those essential, streamlined, non-value-added activities that are necessary to run the business, the solution is to automate these required activities as fully as possible.
- **Manual:** Most processes contain a great number of manual activities, and this is often the case in companies where a computer system has not been custom fitted to the environment. The degree of waste is directly proportional to the mismatch between the computer system and the environment it is intended to serve. A typical example is office personnel spending hours extracting information from the computer, and then manually performing calculations or some other activity by hand. Environments loaded with manual activities are easy to recognize: As the volume of work increases, the staffing level increases proportionately.
- **Not innovative:** This happens because so many companies try to emulate companies with a reputation for success. Sometimes, this mimicry is unintentional—it is an unanticipated and undesired consequence of using commercial off-the-shelf software. The root cause issue, however, is the communication gap between the users of the system and the information technology (IT) department. In most companies, the IT department has the capability to make a competitive difference through a host of system enhancement options, without changing source code (a group of commands created by the software developer that is used to generate an executable program). Unfortunately, this capability is often underutilized because of a communication gap between IT and users who may have a pressing need for system enhancements but are unable to explain what it is they need.

IT personnel are typically highly skilled at programming and maintaining the hardware and software components of the system; they may not be skilled as system analysts. A number of them also feel uncomfortable defining (from a process or program standpoint) what users require. That, after all, is not typically their primary function. Their primary function is to maintain the system and ensure it is up and running properly. The job of defining the required process should rest in the hands of a cross-functional business process improvement team, consisting of users and IT personnel, operating on a top-level direction (strategic objective). This type of team, however, is rare and almost nonexistent in companies that rely on commercial off-the-shelf software, which dictates processes that need to be put into place in order to make the software function. End result? Little to no innovation, processes that do not fit the needs of the environment, and a system whose main value often constitutes nothing more than data retention. All these issues, however, can be dealt with by applying administration automation in leaning the office.

Setting Up the Lean Office

Lean office objectives are the same as those of lean manufacturing: to eliminate waste and reduce non-value-added activities significantly while focusing on required activities that add value to the customer and are necessary to run the business. The distinction between the lean office and lean manufacturing is that required activities in the lean office are automated, elevating office personnel from performing mundane repetitious tasks to performing strategic activities.

There are currently two basic approaches when attempting to create a lean office. The first is applying lean manufacturing techniques, and the second is using commercial off-the-shelf software.

Applying Lean Manufacturing Techniques to the Office

Lean manufacturing techniques are highly effective on the shop floor, and their application is straightforward as designed. When it comes to the office, the application of lean manufacturing techniques is not as straightforward and, in a number of cases, not applicable. The following examples explain this concept.

Load-Smoothing Example

In the manufacturing environment, customer demand is often nonlinear. The objective, however, is to provide a linear build while satisfying customer demand within customer expectations. This objective can be accomplished in certain manufacturing environments by carrying finished goods inventory that serves as a shock absorber during high periods of customer demand. Finished goods inventory permits the shop floor to achieve and maintain a linear build while satisfying customer expectations.

Applying load smoothing to the office has limitations. For example, requests for quotes (RFQs) coming into the original equipment manufacturer's (OEM's) quote department are not linear. These requests come in at random times, and both the quantities and content are unique—the quote department deals with different terms and conditions, quantities, part numbers, and customer-imposed deadlines. This nonlinear workload cannot be offset by having custom RFQs sitting on the shelf.

Kanban Example

In manufacturing, a predetermined quantity is at the point of use, and consumption triggers replenishment. This is referred to as a *pull system* that coordinates the shop and supply base as a whole. This technique has limited application in the office, as there are no predetermined quantities of any specific function or completed task residing on hand. RFQs, as an example, are completed on scheduled due dates that match a customer's deadline for receiving a completed packet.

Quick Changeover Example

Reducing changeover time on the shop floor is paramount in achieving a one-piece flow. Here a quick changeover chart is employed listing all the key elements (steps) of the current setup process. Each of the elements is classified as being internal (what must be done while the machine is shut down) and external (what can be done while the machine is running). The objective is to move internal elements to external elements where appropriate and then streamline the external elements. The end result is reduced setup time. In the office, we are not dealing with machines, but the objective of targeting and reducing setup times is the same as the following example about loan processing illustrates.

Each loan processor in a savings and loan company is responsible for processing a multitude of loan packets that are maintained next to his or her individual workstations. There are numerous steps in processing a loan, and those steps must be performed at specific points in time. There is a flurry of activity to process each loan, as documents are ordered at specific times and are then received and processed. Once the processor completes a task on a loan packet file, it is set aside until the next step in the process needs to take place. The loan processor then searches through all the remaining loan packets he or she is responsible for to determine which one needs to be worked on next. The individual task he or she performs, on average, may take only a couple of minutes, but it takes five or ten minutes to determine which item to work on next. This is a typical pattern that occurs throughout the day and is currently understood to be the norm within the industry.

This process of going from one loan packet to another could be looked upon as a setup time issue. The elimination of waste, however, does not involve applying a quick changeover chart. Instead, changeover time is eliminated through automating the scheduling process. In this example, one sheet of paper is generated from a computer twice a day and is given to each loan processor, specifying which loans need to be worked on that day and which specific tasks need to be done. The computer generates only those items that are ready to be worked on and are due to be completed that day. The concept of setup time being waste is useful in identifying waste. However, it is the application of administration automation techniques that eliminates the waste in the office.

Other Lean Manufacturing Techniques

Some aspects of lean manufacturing are viable in an office environment, for example, some forms of process mapping, root cause analysis, standardization, and the visual factory. But beyond understanding the current process, determining root cause issues, standardizing the work for repeatability, and visually organizing the office, these standard lean manufacturing techniques do not fully address waste elimination in the office or lead to significant improvements. Instead, the primary technique for fully eliminating waste, streamlining non-value-added activities, and gaining significant competitive advantage in the office is computer automation of required activities.

Commercial Off-the-Shelf Software

Just as lean manufacturing techniques are being considered to eliminate waste in the office so is off-the-shelf software. There are numerous software offerings in the market, geared toward every aspect of the office. Each claims to yield a competitive advantage. There are limitations, however, that must be taken into consideration with commercial, standard, off-the-shelf software:

- The software often forces the business to change its business processes dictated by the software package, with little latitude. Any innovative processes already put in place by the business—ones that create a competitive differentiation—may be lost, and the organization risks becoming another "me, too" company.

- A number of software packages attempt to employ best practices. But these methodologies are typically not creative approaches; instead, they are an emulation of best practices used by a few innovative companies, perhaps many years ago. Adopting what everyone else is doing or what someone else did awhile ago does not necessarily lead to a competitive advantage. It is best to be the company that innovates.

- The solutions offered by the software houses may not necessarily be suitable for your specific environment. Take, for example, an automated kanban system that is designed to calculate kanban lot sizes. If the demand is not perfectly linear, the software must have the capability to detect nonlinear demand patterns and compensate for them during the calculation process. This feature is not always available in software packages that calculate kanban lot sizes, and its absence can lead to frequent stockouts.

- Software solutions often create or contribute to non-value-added activities because the software is designed to be applicable to as many different environments as possible. This, combined with solutions that are not a good match for your environment, can make the software a poor investment that is not fully utilized, because users will apply only certain portions of the system while circumventing others. Several years after implementing a highly expensive ERP system, for example, one large OEM found it could not react quickly enough to customer demand and had to create a special department whose sole mission was to "go around the system" to make things happen.

This is not meant to suggest that there are no advantages to procuring and applying off-the-shelf software packages; a number of companies have found them beneficial. What it should suggest, however, is that off-the-shelf software solutions are often limited in creating a competitive advantage and can seriously impact a company if an incorrect selection is made. Commercial off-the-shelf software remains as a viable system enhancement option after processes have been created reflecting required activities, which are then translated into key system requirements specifying required software capabilities. This is discussed in more detail later in this book.

Additional Key Points

- A lean office can withstand a surge in volume, in most cases, without incident and without adding staff. This is a result of constructing processes that have eliminated waste and have reduced non-value-added activities to remaining "required activities" which are then automated. The computer easily handles the spike in workload in most cases.
- Most companies currently have all the basics in place to create a lean office. This entails a computer system, a programmer who is highly familiar with the current system, a business process improvement team, and the tools and methods discussed in this text.

Administration Automation

2

Creating a lean office is a rewarding experience. It offers opportunities to eliminate waste and reduce non-value-added activities, and then provides the capability to automate the balance of required activities. Administration automation creates a multiplier effect, elevating the staff from performing repetitious tasks to performing strategic-level activities, further enhancing the competitive position of the company through innovative ways of servicing customers. From this general overview of administration automation, we can move to definitions and examples that provide the foundation required to understand lean office.

Defining Administration Processes

Administration processes typically consist of a series of tasks that lead toward an intended result, both in the creation and delivery of value to a customer and in the effective perpetuation of a business entity. In other words, each process is designed to accomplish an intended result. The *intended* result may be to design a product, collect funds, or pay suppliers. When analyzing current processes or designing new processes, the intended result is the objective to be accomplished, and all activity making up the process must effectively lead to its realization.

It is also important to understand that there are two types of administration processes and that both are equally valuable. No business entity can survive with only one or the other.

- The first type of process concentrates on creating and delivering value to the customer. This may include processes such as engineering the customer's product in accordance to customer specifications.
- The second type of administration process perpetuates the business. This may include invoicing, payroll, and setting up new employees into the system.

Both types of processes have intended results and are candidates for lean office. (See examples in Figure 2-1.)

Administration Processes	Intended Results
Product Design Process	Creation of product offering for customer.
Order Entry Process	Inform company of customer requirements to initiate action and confirm the transaction with the customer.
Procurement Process	Acquire the necessary items to build the product, service the customer, or maintain company assets.
Scheduling Process	Coordinate activities to deliver the service or product on time.
Shipping Process	Transport the required items to the appropriate destination on time.
Accounts Payable Process	Pay suppliers for product or services rendered.
Accounts Receivable Process	Collect funds for delivering value to the customer.
Hiring Process	Acquire the talent necessary to deliver value to the customer and/or to perpetuate the business.

Figure 2-1. Example of Administration Processes Intended Results

Defining Tasks

A *task* performs a specific function of a process and consists of a series of operations. (See Figures 2-2 and 2-3.)

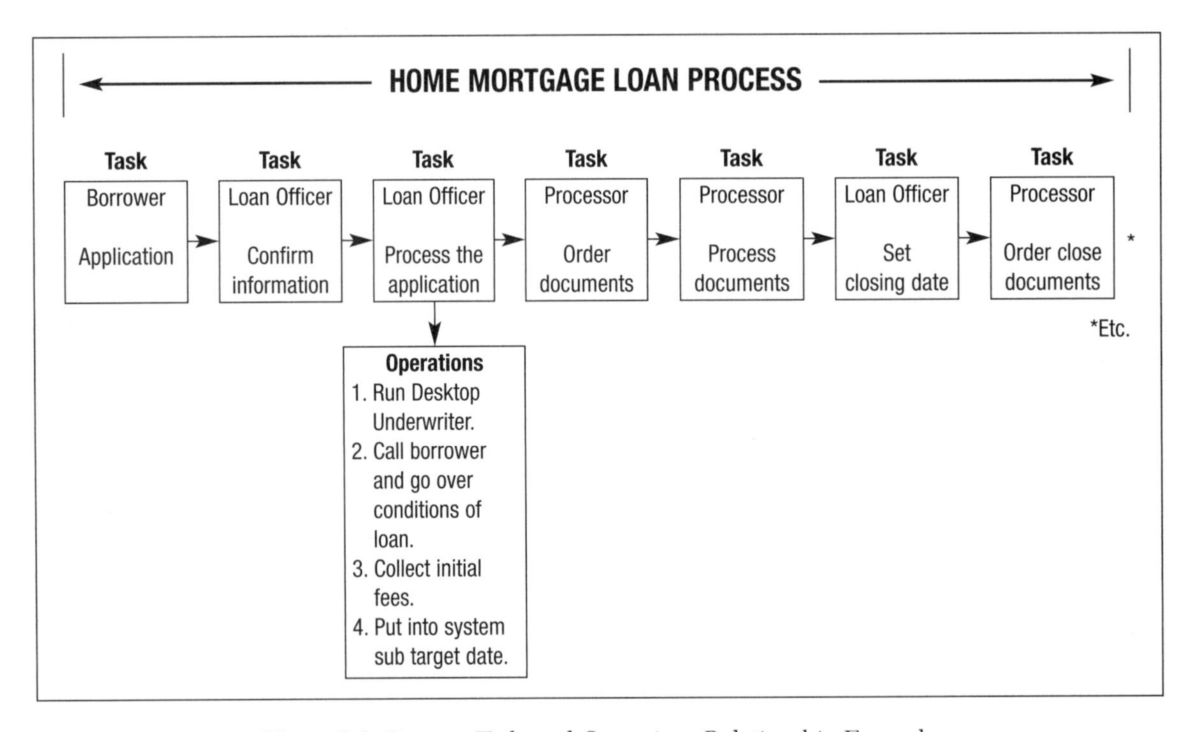

Figure 2-2. Process, Task, and Operations Relationship Example

Tasks are major milestone events that, when performed in sequence, accomplish the intended result of the process. In a lean office, segmenting a process by tasks breaks it down into bite-size, step-by-step portions.

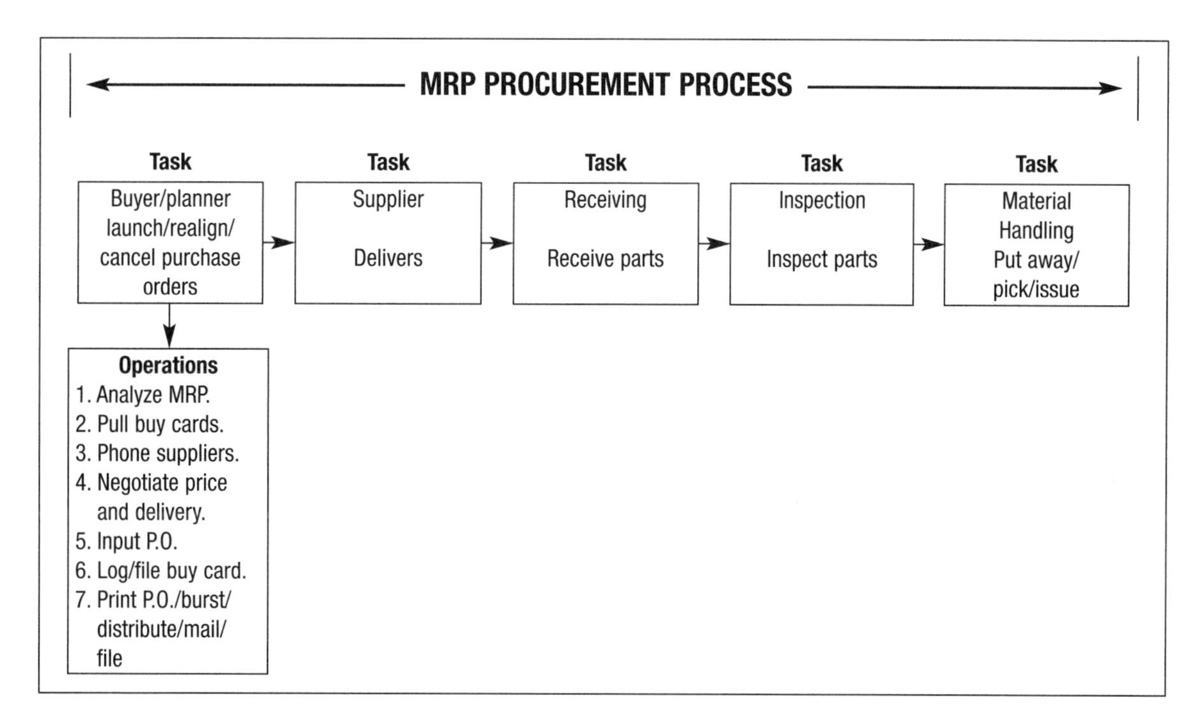

Figure 2-3. Process, Task, and Operations Relationship Example

Each task must accomplish a specific function. Without this structure, we would have only a string of activities listed under the name of a given process and no understanding of what each activity is trying to accomplish. Thus, tasks are individual milestone events, performed in sequence, accomplishing a respective function, which leads to the intended result of the process.

Defining an Operation

An *operation* is a specific activity that supports performing a task. (Refer to Figures 2-2 and 2-3.) Operations are individual steps reflected in sequence that accomplish an individual task. This structure (process→task→operation) is the key to assessing current processes, developing new processes, designing new routines, and defining the key requirements of off-the-shelf software.

Defining Required Activities

Required activities are the remaining activities of a process that has eliminated waste and reduced non-value-added activities to the absolute minimum. Required activities consist of 1) value-added activities that create value for the customer, and 2) essential non-value-added activities that are required to run the business. Required activities are automated (using computers) to the fullest extent possible.

Defining the Lean Office

A lean office consists of processes that have eliminated waste, minimized non-value-added activities, corrected performance issues, integrated disjointed processes, and automated required activities. Leaning an office creates a rapid, accurate, and cost effective means of delivering superior value to the customer and effectively perpetuating the business.

Defining Administration Automation

Administration automation is the application of system enhancement options that automate required activities. The conversion to a lean office is driven by strategic objectives. A lean office is a powerful competitive tool that must be in alignment with the direction of the company. Implementing the lean office is a highly coordinated event, with all departments understanding the direction the company is moving in and participating as required in the lean office effort. Implementation is not a continuous improvement event performed by multiple teams doing multiple projects—such as minimizing the distance to the copier or controlling office supplies. Instead, it is a sequence of carefully structured administration automation techniques capable of eliminating waste, minimizing non-value-added activities, correcting performance issues, and integrating disjointed processes. Administration automation is also employed to create and utilize innovative techniques that create superior value for customers and competitive differentiation.

Defining Performance Issue(s)

A *performance issue* is any impediment to satisfying customer expectations or perpetuating the business effectively in terms of speed, accuracy, costs, level of service, and timeliness of completion. The impediment is the root cause issue. When a strategic objective is given in regard to a performance issue, a root cause analysis is performed to determine the affected process (or processes). The affected process is then corrected or reinvented to eliminate the root cause issue(s).

Defining Disjointed Processes

A *disjointed process* is a process that transcends departmental/company boundaries, with no specific "owner(s)" assigned responsibility for effectively accomplishing its intended result. Disjointed processes often create communication issues within and beyond the organization. Moreover, disjointed processes are often characterized by departments concerned with performing their individual respective task(s) rather than being concerned with the intended result of the overall process. (See Figure 2-4 for examples.)

- **Request for Quote Process:** Encompasses legal, sales, product managers, finance, etc.
- **Procurement Process:** Encompasses sales forecasting, master scheduling, material planning, purchasing, suppliers, receiving, inspection, material handling.
- **Home Loan Process:** Encompasses loan officer, processors, closing, funding.

Figure 2-4. Disjointed Process Examples

Defining the Multiplier Effect

The *multiplier effect* is the expansion of value that occurs when the administrative work force is elevated from performing manual tasks to strategic-level activities. Many office workers perform repetitious, mundane tasks that inspire little if any job satisfaction and can eventually lead to serious discontentment. This type of work also significantly impedes the development of the office workforce and has a negative impact on creativity. When waste is eliminated and non-value-added activities are streamlined, only required activities remain; automating these required activities creates a multiplier effect and numerous positive changes in work as well as attitude about work. (See Figures 2-5a, 2-5b, and 2-5c.)

PURCHASING DEPARTMENT	
Task Oriented	**Strategic Activities**
• Launching and realigning purchase orders. • Shortage meetings, expediting. • Short-term contracts, competitive bidding.	• Forming long-term partnerships and strategic alliances of a global nature. • Sourcing. • Value analysis. • Awareness and application of technological innovations. • Developing commodity strategies. • Make versus buy analysis. • Align the activities of the supply base to reduce waste, cost, and time. • Concurrent engineering. • Reduction of the supply base.

Figure 2-5a. Purchasing Department Multiplier Effect Examples

SALES	
Task Oriented	**Strategic Activities**
• Manually developing forecast. • Determining missed sales opportunities. • Tracking shipment dollars by customer for price breaks per the contract. • Determining sales commissions based upon dollar amount customers purchased. • Determining potential sales opportunities.	• Service the customer more directly and acquire market intelligence for new products & services. • Work with the customers to define "value." • Develop software enabling the sales force to prepare and submit complex quotations while on customer premises. • Identify profitable and unprofitable customers.

Figure 2-5b. Sales Department Multiplier Effect Examples

HOME LOAN PROCESSORS	
Task Oriented	**Strategic Activities**
• Looking through each loan folder to determine what to work on next. • Looking through the system on each loan to see what loan documents are still due and expedite.	• Work with loan officers in responding to loan inquiries to increase sales capture rate.

Figure 2-5c. Home Loan Processors Multiplier Effect Examples

The Thirteen Types of Office Waste

Waste is any activity other than required activities (which have already been automated to the fullest extent possible). There are thirteen types of waste that are prevalent in the office; they are discussed in the following sections.

The seven steps of administration automation employ a team-based tool to create processes consisting only of required activities. In determining these required activities, the thirteen types of waste are taken into consideration. The remaining required activities are then looked at from an automation standpoint. This is covered in detail in Chapter 13.

Disjointed Processes

Disjointed processes create delays in sending, receiving, and analyzing information. They also create a void in responsibility for achieving the intended result of the overall process. Assume, for example, that the production control department is trying to manually construct a manufacturing build schedule based upon the sales forecast being manually developed by each of the multiple company-owned distribution centers. Without automating the sales forecasts for each distribution site, this project is likely to be subjected to numerous delays, miscommunication or issues with inaccurate oral or written information especially if each distribution site carries hundreds of part numbers. An automated process could create and present the forecasts for approval for each distribution center, determine appropriate stocking levels for each site as compared with their respective current on-hand inventory to determine replenishment timing, and appropriate replenishment quantities for each part number by distribution site. The automated system could then use that, and other information contained in the computer, to automatically create the manufacturing schedule for review or adjustment, as required.

Manual Repetitious Activity

Manual repetitious activity creates needless costs and delays. An example is opening work orders for individually booked items. When this task is performed manually, the work orders are not created immediately and at times are overlooked altogether creating a need for overtime and expediting. Manual repetitious activities are ideal for automation.

Incorrect Techniques

Incorrect techniques means applying methods inappropriate for the environment. An example is employing an MRP procurement methodology to an environment that is, instead, ideal for kanban. Techniques that are not suitable for the environment in which they are employed generate numerous unneeded activities. For example, each time the MRP is generated a tremendous amount of realignments and cancellations to open purchase orders and factory work orders may have to take place due to the nervousness of the system. However, if kanban were applied, realignments would not be required.

Wait Time

Wait time comes in many forms, but typical examples include waiting for approval or other information before being able to complete the task or process.

Searching

Searching is trying to determine what should be worked on next or whether everything required to begin and perform work is available. An example is processing multiple projects without knowing what should be worked on that day, by whom, and whether the worker(s) will have the necessary data, authorization, or documents to proceed.

Unresolved Impediments

Unresolved impediments refers to anything that impacts the speed, accuracy, cost, level of service, and timeliness of completion. Impediments are root cause issues that have not been resolved.

Performing Obsolete Processes, Tasks, and Operations

Obsolete processes, tasks, and operations need to be identified and eliminated. These are activities that once had a purpose but are no longer required. Assume, for example, that a worker is checking revision levels on each finish goods item (prior to shipping), and is engaging an activity that is no longer required because the root cause issue of having out-of-revision finish goods in stock has been eliminated.

Producing Ahead Of or Behind Schedule

Producing ahead of schedule is a waste of resource, as the time should be spent on what is currently due. *Working behind schedule* causes other inefficiencies, such as costly overnight shipments, overtime, overtaxing other resources to make up for lost time, and so on.

Duplication of Effort

Duplication of effort is doing the same task twice. Examples include rekeying the same information into the computer or having two different departments perform the same operations, tasks, or processes.

Multiple Computer Screens to Acquire or Enter Data

Too often, commercial off-the-shelf software is designed without thought to minimizing non-value-added activities. The most typical generic issue is that the user is forced to access multiple computer screens to acquire or enter data. This can have a serious impact when it comes to repetitive tasks. A good example is a person who is entering customer orders and must go to multiple screens to determine product availability, pricing, agreed-upon contracted terms, shipping address, and billing address.

Improper Staffing

Improper staffing means that the workload in the office—expressed in hours, by date, and by person—is unknown. Staffing in this situation is a guesstimate at best, and this can lead to overstaffing or understaffing, which leads to wasted human and financial resources. Consider, for example, what is likely to happen when an office is processing customer orders (mortgage, escrow, custom manufactured goods, landscaping projects), and no one knows if there is enough capacity to handle the workload. Typical results are late customer orders, excess overtime, emergency overnight shipments, and a demoralized staff. Noticing how many files are stacked on the floor or on desks is *not* enough; it is essential to know the workload expressed in hours versus the number of people available to do it.

Lack of Innovation

Lack of innovation—that is, depending upon the creativity of others in the industry to show the path to new methodologies—is asking for failure. The methods employed by the innovative company are tailored to their specific environment. Emulation without knowing the particulars can have serious consequences. Of concern is not applying ones own creativity in creating competitive differentiation while at the same time minimizing waste and non-value-added activities beyond industry standards.

Talent Loss

Talent loss is, without question, the greatest of all wastes. People in most offices are performing mundane repetitious activities versus performing strategic-level activities. By automating these processes, the people are elevated from performing these repetitious tasks to performing strategic-level activities, which further enhances the competitive position of the company.

Environmental Factors

The designs of processes are greatly influenced by an organization's strategy and by environmental factors. The strategy dictates the company's direction by way of strategic objectives that must be achieved. This, more often than not, requires that processes must be changed or new processes must be created. Each company's environmental factors dictate specific process design.

Environmental factors are the operating conditions of the business. Typically, they are unique for each company—even competitors who make the same product or render the same service often have different environmental factors requiring different processes. Examples of such differences are presented in the following sections.

Linearity of Customer Demand

Some environments experience linear customer demand, so they have little trouble meeting customer expectations (from a workload standpoint) and require no special capability. Other environments experience nonlinear customer demand, requiring specialized processes or capabilities. Such a company might, for example, need to know the demand expressed in hours for a given process, in order to shift crossed-trained staff to the areas that have encountered high levels of demand.

Product and Service Customization

A standard off-the-shelf final product requires different processes than a customized product. For example, for a manufacturing environment, the following administration processes would be affected: bidding, order entry, costing, forecasting, master scheduling, procurement, and production scheduling. Even in pure service industries, the level and type of service required for each customer may differ.

Government Regulations

There are certain paperwork requirements that must be adhered to in specific industries. For example, the Federal Aviation Administration (FAA) requires compliance in Airworthiness Approval Tags (a record-keeping device that declares that an identified item is airworthy). These regulations must be taken into consideration in any new process design.

Coordination Levels

Coordination of a process is greatly simplified when it is confined to a specific department. The greater the number of departments involved, the more complex the process becomes. Taking this a step further, the complexity grows exponentially if the departments are located in different companies or countries.

A complete list of environmental factors would be well beyond the scope of this book. The intent here is to make the reader aware of the importance of environmental factors when creating new processes or modifying current processes and to point out why standard off-the-shelf solutions cannot, in most cases, meet the needs of most companies. In fact, no standard off-the-shelf package can handle all the environmental factors of all companies. The net result of attempting to use such a package without customization follows:

- Current processes do not match what is required for the company to compete effectively because the processes that are put into place must match the dictates of the software package. Common sense dictates that any software "solution" should meet the strategic needs and environmental factors of the company, not the other way around.
- The "system" in many cases is not fully employed by the users, because it does not provide what is required. The user performs many tasks manually, finding value mainly in using the computer as a database and not in the operational programs. This is a major problem for many companies.
- The company, at best, becomes another "me too" contender. The winner, more often than not, is the company whose competitive strategy and environmental factors happen to be better aligned with the software package process requirements. No

company can buy its way into being a world class performer. World class companies are built from the ground up through good leadership and innovation.

The Evolution from Performing Task Activities to Performing Strategic Activities

The degree of firefighting in environments that have not created a lean office is high. The situation becomes worse when a spike in workload occurs. Spikes in demand will occur regardless of whether the processes are automated; however, in a lean office, the computer can handle the shifts in volume far better than a single person or even a group of people, typically without incident. To create a lean office, three key elements are required:

- New processes need to be created that
  - are in alignment with the strategy and environmental factors of the company;
  - contain new methodologies to achieve a competitive advantage;
  - have eliminated waste and streamlined non-value-added activities and consist only of required activities.
- The required activities need to be automated to the fullest extent possible.
- Impediments creating performance issues need to be resolved.

The degree to which companies have achieved a lean office can be gauged by using a four-tiered scale shown in Figure 2-6. Each level is explained in the following sections.

Level 1: Constant Firefight Mode

This is the worst operating level, so it is easy to identify. The office appears disorganized, and the staff is working extremely hard, putting out fires. The root cause issue is not a lack of organization but rather the lack of the application of the three key elements discussed in the preceding sections. Most companies fall in a Level 1 or Level 2 rating.

Level 2: Task Oriented

This is the second worst level and is also easy to identify. It has the same root cause issues as firefighting, but is not as bad because the system is more compatible with the company strategy and environmental factors. Very little is accomplished in this environment unless it is manually attended to. The staff is in a constant overtime mode, because overtime is used to compensate for the root cause issues. When a spike in workload occurs, overtime is required to avoid major problems. When a spike in workload subsides, overtime is required to catch up on the less-pressing activities that were set aside to handle the spike.

Level 3: Improvement Oriented

At this level, lean office through administration automation has been initiated in areas that need major improvement. This automation is guided by strategic objectives. As the level of manual tasks subsides, overtime is greatly reduced and strategic activities are employed to further enhance the competitive position of the company.

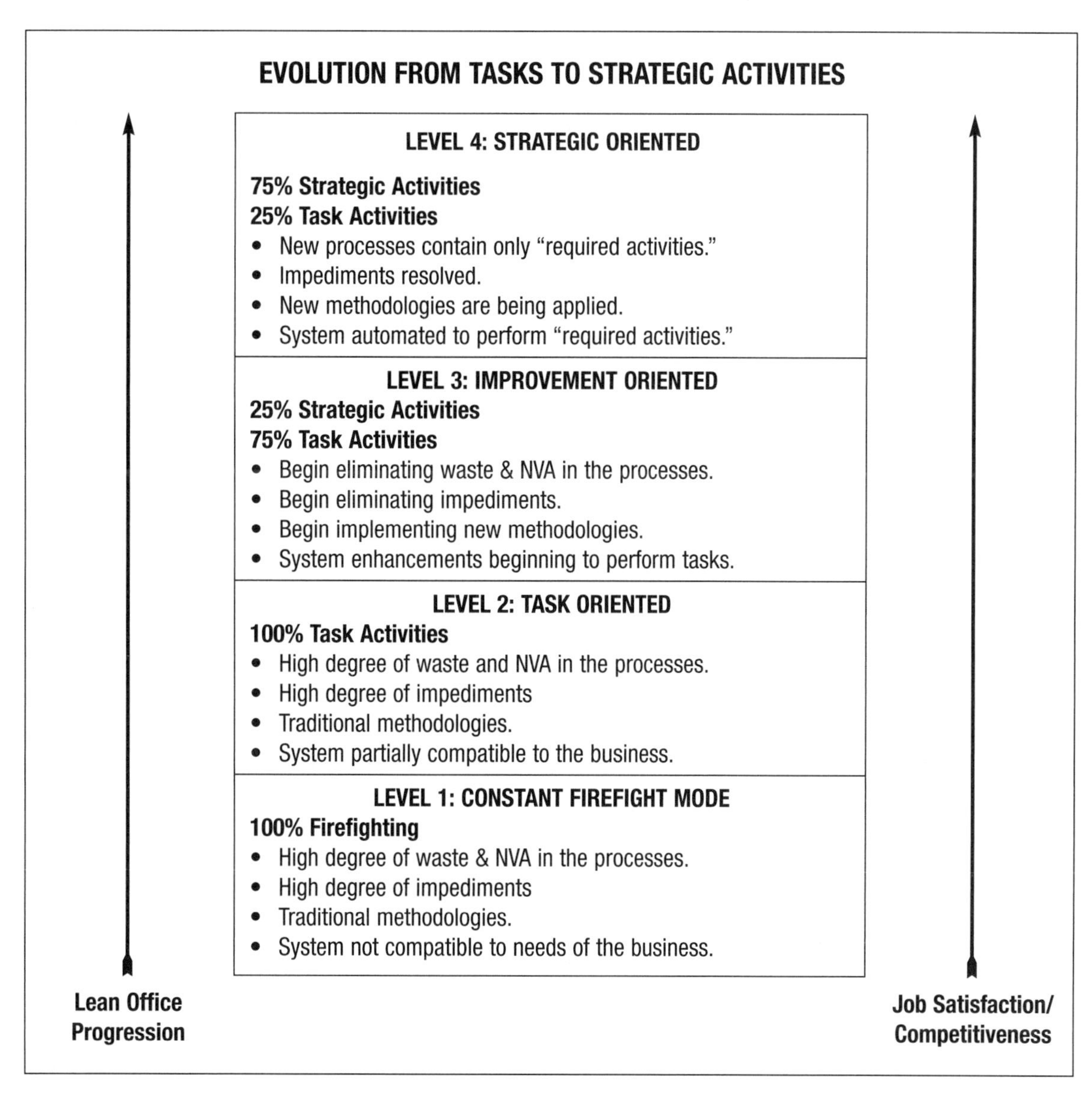

Figure 2-6. Evolution From Task to Strategic Activities

Level 4: Strategic Oriented

The office has been fully converted into a lean office by applying the seven steps to administration automation. Strategic activities represent the bulk of activities now performed, and the job satisfaction and competitiveness of the company have greatly improved.

Additional Key Points

- Simply automating existing processes without eliminating waste and streamlining non-value-added activities can do more harm than good. It may literally be doing the wrong things faster.

- Your processes are too important to have an off-the-shelf software package dictate what they should look like. Your processes are what separate you from your competitors; if they are not efficient, they are the root cause of failure to compete successfully with other companies. If you are contemplating using an external software package, you must define your key requirements, and then select the software package that meets these criteria. This is covered in Chapter 4.

Automating Administration Processes

3

The number of administration processes that can be automated is immense—take a look at examples in Figure 3-1. Automation focuses on the remaining required activities. When each operation and task within a process is automated, the process as a whole becomes automated.

Manufacturing	Distribution	Service (Savings & Loan Example)
• Scheduling & tracking quotes. • Booking customer orders. • Customer credit check. • Generating a forecast. • Creating a master production schedule. • Determining kanban lot size. • Triggering requirements. • Expediting. • Launching and realigning MRP orders. • Providing status to the customer. • Generating shippers. • Invoicing. • Measuring performance. • Paying invoices.	• Determining location of product. • Determining staffing requirements. • Determining min/max. • Generating a forecast. • Capacity planning. • Booking customer orders. • Providing status to the customer. • Generating shippers. • Triggering requirements. • Expediting. • Processing receipts. • Measuring performance. • Determining slow moving & obsolete. • Paying invoices. • Determining lost sales due to lack of corrective action.	• Scheduling each person of the loan process daily. • Ordering documents. • Expediting documents. • Reviewing documents. • Document payments. • Providing status to the customer. • Tracking & exception reporting. • Measuring performance. • Determining employee workload. • Capacity planning.

Figure 3-1. Task Automation Examples

Source Code Changes

The source code is a group of commands created by the system software developer used to generate an executable program. Often, the automation of processes does not entail source code changes. An IT representative is part of the business process improvement (BPI) team that participates in the assessment of current processes and development of new processes by applying the seven steps of administration automation. Once the new processes are defined, reflecting the required activities, the system enhancement(s) are selected, enabling the IT staff to apply its skill.

Applying Continuous Improvement

Continuous improvement is an exceptionally valuable approach to improving processes on the shop floor. Additional gains are achieved in effectiveness as lean manufacturing techniques that have been implemented continue to be honed, yielding modest but important gains in effectiveness. Continuous improvement is different than an initial full implementation of lean manufacturing techniques, which can be classified as nothing less than a full conversion, where each of the lean manufacturing techniques are systematically implemented throughout the shop floor based on the strategic needs of the company.

The reason strategic needs are addressed first in lean manufacturing is that it takes several years to fully implement all the lean manufacturing techniques on the shop floor. The shopfloor conversion effort must first focus on what is deemed vital for the company's well being. If it is determined, for example, that customer on-time delivery needs to be elevated from 33 percent to 99 percent within three months, a root cause analysis is performed to identify the root cause issue(s), which are then addressed. For example, the root cause analysis may determine that the manufacturing lead times to respond to customer demand is the main issue for having a 33 percent customer on-time rate. Knowing the root cause issue(s) then leads to the specific lean manufacturing technique(s) that need to be put into place immediately. It may be determined that internal kanban with work cell implementation is the lean manufacturing technique that needs to be implemented now.

If it were left up to the continuous improvement teams to select what they want without knowing external factors, one group may be implementing total productive maintenance, another group may be implementing visual factory, and another group may be focusing on concurrent engineering. Instead of this misguided approach, lean manufacturing conversions are often driven by strategic objectives.

The full conversion effort for the administration office is applied in the same manner. The upper echelon must drive it because they know the industry, competitors, customer's requirements, and their own current performance levels. From this external and internal assessment, a strategy is formed and strategic objectives are defined, initiating a root cause analysis that identifies the key office processes that need to be improved. This is absolutely vital in understanding what needs to be done, by when, and in what order.

Seven Steps of Administration Automation

There is a prescribed methodology for creating a lean office: the seven steps of administration automation. Figure 3-2 provides a brief primer; Part Three covers the seven steps in detail.

Figure 3-2 reveals that this step-by-step method begins with performing an external/internal analysis, determining strategy, and stating strategic objectives. Alternatively, this

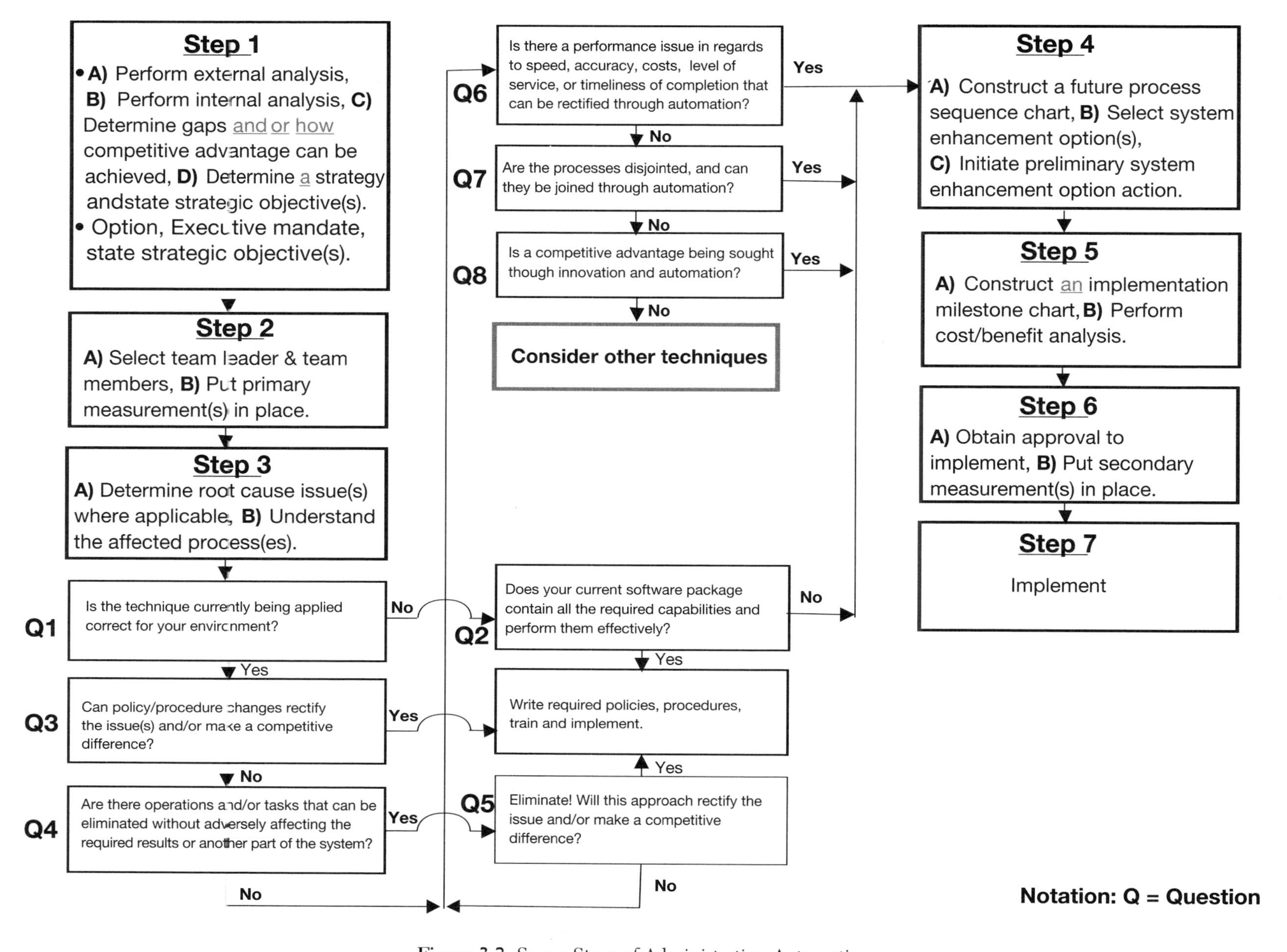

Figure 3-2. Seven Steps of Administration Automation

first step can be an executive mandate, requiring specific accomplishments, which is also driven by stated strategic objectives. In either case, the process requires a BPI team whose charter is to accomplish the strategic objectives. It determines root cause issue(s) where applicable, understanding of affected processes, and poses key questions at the appropriate time to the team concerning the current techniques being applied to the environment, and questions if policies and procedures may lead to solutions that are not typically obvious. It further addresses the question of whether administration automation is applicable to the issue being worked on and guides the user through the balance of the steps leading to the creation of new processes and application of system enhancements. Top-level management is responsible for driving this seven-step process, as it is within management's scope of duties to be familiar with external and internal factors that affect an organization and to formulate a strategy reflecting this knowledge. A shift in strategy typically requires that the processes shift accordingly to support the new or modified strategic objective(s).

This seven-step methodology has been applied to companies grossing from $12 million to $10 billion annually. In addition, the scope of application varies from rectifying impediments (for example, reducing a 35.0 percent part shortage rate to 0.25 percent) to designing and implementing fully automated supply chain systems involving foreign and domestic distributors with multiple manufacturing sites to working with pure service industries. A few examples follow.

Example #1: Mortgage Banking Company

Midwest Loan Services is located in the upper peninsula of Michigan. The company processes new mortgage loans for credit unions and individual customers. It also services existing loans (processes mortgage payments). Company management decided to apply lean office (administration automation) to the processing of new home mortgage loans.

Symptoms

Based on industry standards, Midwest Loan Services was as good as most of its competitors. However, the company wanted to be better than its competition and also wanted to excel in handling unexpected large swings in business that occur on home loans when interest rates fluctuate, a situation that routinely affects the industry.

Tools in Place

Before changing to lean office, the company was using a standard loan processing system that tracked the loan packet in regard to what activities were completed. It had limited scheduling and process control capability, although it had the ability to allow the user to electronically order required documents when they were needed.

Lean Office Solutions

Many changes occurred as lean office was implemented. The following list describes a few of the enhancements that were put into place:

- **Policy Enacted:** A new policy changed the way documents received in the mailroom were handled. As documents arrived, receipt was recorded into the system and then each document was delivered to the appropriate person the same day it was received. This eliminated the need for office staff to spend time determining whether documents had been received.
- **Automated Scheduling System:** This system was designed specifically for the environment. It scheduled by date each required activity that had to be performed. The system would print out a one-page report for each employee, specifying the loan number, activity required, and estimated hours of work that had to be completed that day. Only those items scheduled to be completed that day and were ready to be worked on are reflected. This eliminated the repetitious search after each employee performed a task, to determine which loan packet was to be worked on next. It typically took five to ten minutes to search through all the loan packets, while it only took a few minutes to perform the required activities.
- **Summary of Hours Report:** A one-page report was generated daily reflecting the workload expressed in hours for each person. This report was used by the supervisor to shift cross-trained personnel to overload areas and was used to determine overtime, if required. This maximized the effectiveness of each employee.
- **Loan Processing Exception Report:** Any loan in process that missed a specific task completion date appeared on this one-page report. It identified the loan number, task that fell behind, and the employee assigned to the task. This permitted intervention to resolve any issue prior to impact.
- **Document Expedite Report:** Any document that was past due appeared on this one-page report for immediate action.
- **Executive Dashboard:** All key measurements were available on the system with a few clicks of the mouse. This included the percentage of loans in process that were running on time, the percentage of loans completed on time, projected load in hours as compared with current staffing hours, documents received on time, number of leads being worked on by the loan officers, and so on.

These and the many other enhancements that were put into place 1) reduced waste, 2) reduced non-value-added activities, and 3) applied new methodologies. The end result is that the new system (which the company calls RPM, or Rapid Processing Method) reduced the average time to process loans by 60 percent, significantly improved the effectiveness of the staff, increased the on-time completion of loans, and prepared the operation to handle swings in business volume more efficiently.

Example #2: Manufacturer with Company-Owned Foreign and Domestic Distribution Centers

This business had two manufacturing sites and ten company-owned foreign and domestic distribution centers, offered over 950 end items, and utilized a legacy MRPII system.

This system, based at company headquarters, had electronic connectivity to the other manufacturing plant and distribution centers.

Symptoms

- Lost sales opportunities due to lack of on-shelf availability
- Low overall inventory turn ratio
- Excessive drop shipments (from one distribution center to another to satisfy the needs of the customer)
- Excessive lag time in developing and responding to forecasted requirements

Root Cause Issues

- Forecasts were exceptionally time-consuming to develop, as they were created manually and required input and coordination among all facilities (disjointed processes). As a result, the forecasts were not produced and put into effect until the changes in the marketplace were already well underway (lack of speed and timeliness of completion impediments).
- Inaccurate forecasts stemming from hand calculations (accuracy impediment).
- Lack of policy and procedures or a standard method to determine what quantities should be maintained on the distribution centers' shelves and what quantities should be ordered when triggers occurred. Each distribution center had its own way of determining its requirements. Some employed correct methodologies; others did not. There was a direct correlation between the distribution centers that were incorrectly calculating shelf and order quantities and those that required a high degree of excessive drop shipments.
- Almost all administration functions were manual. This included hand calculations to determine what should be maintained on the shelf, entering of sales orders from each distribution center to the respective manufacturing sites seeking replenishment, scheduling production, and expediting (repetitious activities and not innovative).

Lean Office Solutions

Lean office solutions included the following:

- Automating the forecasting routine. A forecast specialist would input marketing forecasted dollars by product code and the system would determine a times factor and apply it to historical sales quantities to generate a forecasted quantity for each part number. Forecasts were then reviewed, modified as required for special circumstances, and activated. This automated process completed each forecast (with the review process) within two business days, versus nine business days doing it the old, manual way.
- Automatically calculated stocking levels for all distribution and manufacturing locations, which were then reviewed for special circumstances and activated (standardized methodology).

- Triggering was automated for the distribution centers. Consumption automatically triggered demand, which created and downloaded sales orders to the manufacturing plants.
- Consumption of final product at the manufacturing site stemming from the distribution sales orders automatically triggered demand to the terminals at the work centers responsible for replenishment.
- Expediting was automated through a material simulation program of the triggered demand at each work center. Anticipated shortages were automatically determined and made available on the specific buyer's terminal reflecting the supplier and current open purchase orders. The buyers expedited these items and inputted into the system the expected receive date that was then reflected on the manufacturing work centers' terminals that required the specific item.

End Result

Inventory was reduced 24 percent within a short period of time, drop shipments decreased 63 percent, and sales increased 8 percent due to increased availability of the right item being on the shelf. The OEM eventually purchased an ERP package to help blend this business entity into the corporate entity, mainly from an accounting requirement standpoint. The enhancements detailed in the preceding section were then programmed into the new ERP package by the supplier of the ERP package.

Functions That Can Be Improved through Administration Automation

Almost every function or activity in the office can be aided and/or vastly improved by employing administration automation. This includes:

- Top level management
- Shopfloor improvement teams
- Engineering
- Legal
- Sales
- Order entry
- Master scheduling
- Production scheduling
- Expediting
- Industrial engineers
- Stockroom
- Distribution
- Shipping

- Receiving
- Accounting
- Human resources
- Production supervisors

Example #1: Top Level Management

A great deal of time is often wasted by people trying to extract data manually to determine status. A personalized, tailor-made dashboard of key operating statistics can be put in place for managers, minimizing the wasted time of extracting computer data manually and then following this activity with hand calculations.

Example #2: Shopfloor Improvement Team's Work Cell Development

A shopfloor improvement team was trying to implement work cells in a shop that produced more than 2,500 part numbers. The team had been working on this project for more than four months, trying to determine the number and types of machines required for each work cell and the associated part numbers that would be made in those work cells. After four months' time, team members managed to review only 600 part numbers routings. A simple computer program, capable of assessing all the part numbers within two hours, was designed (in two days) and programmed (in four days). The program:

- Took each manufactured item and acquired the anticipated yearly usage.
- Took what the user defined as high volume part numbers (user inputted one quantity—for example, 2,000 pieces per year, prior to initiating the program) and went through each part number's routing, identifying the machines they went through (in sequence), and captured setup time and run time for each part number/machine. The average run quantities were based upon the one user's input of time (for example, one-day run quantity, two-day run quantity, five-day run quantity, and so on).
- Grouped all the part numbers that went through the same type of machines in the same sequence. It then added all the setup times and run times for each machine for all the part numbers that went through the same series and sequence of machines.

The team used the resulting data to perform a series of what-if analyses. It could add or subtract part numbers that were candidates for the work cell based on the yearly quantity that was defined (by user input) as a high volume part number and adjust the run quantities, which in turn increased or decreased the required capacity. From this report, the teams knew how many work cells were required, the number and types of machines required in each work cell, anticipated workload in hours versus available capacity, and so on.

The report also included all the part numbers that were not candidates for the work cell and determined required machine capacity to ensure that the machines acquired for the work cells would not adversely impact the balance of the part numbers not in work cells.

With this automated report, the shopfloor improvement team was able to determine the required work cells within four weeks. The team then proceeded to perform a focused factory plant layout, which would encompass the positioning of the new work cells.

Example #3: Engineering

A metal shop, which manufactured custom sheet metal products, created a program for the engineering department. This program aided the engineers in designing product and facilitated costing. Each incoming customer order went through engineering for product development. A computer program based on key characteristics of the product guided material selection and cost determination. Once the product was manufactured on the production floor, the actual manufacturing time versus estimated time generated by the program was compared, and parameters for costing were adjusted for accuracy. This program saved engineers a great deal of time, both in product development and product costing.

These are only a few examples of the thousands of ways administration automation can be used to improve office capabilities. Applying this methodology, however, requires an appropriate mindset.

Developing the Appropriate Mindset

There are three main ingredients for successful administration automation. The first is to realize that the ineffective processes would be considered intolerable in a world class company. The second is to understand that your company is not locked in or limited to the capabilities of your current software package and that numerous system enhancement options can be applied yielding significant results. The third is to acknowledge that the only real limitation you face is preconceived notions of what can or cannot be accomplished. A corollary to these key prerequisites is that the distinction between a world class performer and the "me too" group is that the former does not tolerate unacceptable present conditions, takes ownership of the condition, and initiates improvements with a can-do attitude. The "me too" group, on the other hand, wastes time and energy before discovering that following paths mapped by others leads to their destinations, which are shaped by their own limitations and preconceived thoughts. Essentially, you will get out of it what you put into it.

Additional Key Points

- Automation can improve almost every activity performed in a lean office.
- An IT programmer who has intimate knowledge of the computer system should always be part of any business process improvement team that is formed.

PART TWO

System Enhancement Options

The seven steps of administration automation are a powerful toolset that drives improvements in those areas of the office deemed most in need of improvement. It has the capability to identify waste and unnecessary non-value-added activities, which are eliminated and streamlined as new processes consisting only of required activities. The new processes are created by the business process improvement (BPI) team, which then selects the system enhancement option that achieves the goal of automation.

Part Two of *Creating the Ultimate Lean Office* explains how existing or newly created office processes can be automated to meet an organization's strategic and environmental needs. The information provided in Part Two sets the stage for Part Three, which covers the seven steps of administration automation in more detail.

Thus, the chapters included in this section of the book evolve in a manner that presupposes a BPI team has already created a new process consisting of only required activities and now begins to consider the best system enhancement option(s) for automation. The five system enhancement options discussed in this work are software configuration settings, bolt-on, extension, supplier source code modification, and custom routine. The first system enhancement option (software configuration settings) is so simple it requires little explanation and is briefly described below. The other four options are discussed in Chapters 5 through 8.

Software configuration settings are preprogrammed "out-of-the-box" options embedded in the software program. Configuration settings permit some flexibility on how the software will operate, dictated by choices the user makes. As a rule, the level of complexity of configuration settings rises with the complexity of the software itself. Below are some examples of typical configuration settings:

- Apply optional functionality (apply a master schedule program or master production schedule program)
- Change or add to the data input screen (when entering in a sales order, an employee may want to input a contract number)

- Format current system reports (customize an accounting report or select types and styles of reports)
- Apply shipping methods or currency codes

In many software packages, "out-of-the-box" configuration options can be reviewed during the installation and setup process, and IT groups, working with an in-house software consultant, select the options that are most appropriate for the company's needs. At other times, the configuration settings are preset at the software supplier's location, based upon their understanding of the customer requirements. Typically, these preset configuration settings have little to offer from a functional standpoint (for example, a choice to employ a Regenerative MRP or Net Change MRP) but at times, they do exist and assumptions as to their existence should not be made. Configuration settings yielding specific capabilities may exist in the package but are not visible to the user on the computer or even evident in the software documentation. It would take little effort to contact the supplier of the software package to determine whether specific user-defined capabilities exist in the software package.

Often, there is not a lot of opportunities for rectifying major issues or fully automating the required activities through configuration settings; however, once the BPI team has defined the process, the IT representative can investigate configuration settings. Based on this investigation, the team can determine whether configuration settings are a viable system enhancement option for the specific process being considered. The simplest of the five-system enhancement options, software configuration settings does not involve changing source code.

The Bolt-On System Enhancement Option

4

This system enhancement option (also commonly called *plug in, add-on, third party, canned solution, commercial off-the-shelf products, boxed solution*, and *bolt-on*) typically permits companies to purchase and install additional functional capability. For our purposes, we will call this system enhancement option *bolt-on* throughout this text. Bolt-on packages can perform the following functions:

- Sourcing
- Forecasting
- Booking orders
- Gathering total demand from multiple divisions (for supplier negotiation purposes)
- Procuring
- Connecting electronically to trade partners
- Conducting reverse actions
- Designing products
- Production scheduling
- Capacity planning
- Warehousing
- Attending to transportation needs
- Tracking customer orders
- Accounting

As the list above suggests, there are hundreds of bolt-ons, covering every conceivable function. In general, if the fields of information required are unique and numerous, the bolt-on probably comes with its own database. If the fields of information required match those in the main package, the bolt-on may not require its own database and use the database of the main package.

Five Steps to Selecting a Bolt-On

There are five common, basic steps to determine whether a bolt-on product can be integrated with existing hardware and software and perform the required activities that were developed by the business process improvement (BPI) team. The integration requirements and performance of required activities are translated into "key requirements" that the software must satisfy.

Step One: List the Key Requirements

List the key requirements that the bolt-on must meet on a Software Key Requirements Form. (See Figure 4-1.) Key requirements include 1) a listing of current software and hardware that is in place at your facility (this ensures there is not an integration issue with the specific bolt-on being considered), and 2) specific vital functional capabilities of the software that will perform the required activities defined by the BPI team. For example, in Figure 4-1, the BPI team created a list of questions considered to be minimum requirements for the bolt-on selection process. The first item on the list (current computer hardware and software) would be supplemented with an attachment, listing the current hardware and software currently in place.

Page 1 of 2	**SOFTWARE KEY REQUIREMENTS FORM**			Date: 11/16/09
Required Function: Process Home Mortgage Loans				
	Key Requirements	**Suppliers**		
1	Can your software integrate with the attached list of software and hardware?			
2	Does the package have a prequalification calculator?			
3	Does your package download standard forms (e.g., 1003, etc.) and data?			
4	Does your package have automated underwriting capability?			
5	Does the package have more than 25 status fields for tracking?			
6	Does your package have document exception reporting?			
7	Does your package have in-process exception reporting?			

Figure 4-1. Software Key Requirements Form

Step Two: Locate the Best-Known Software Suppliers

Once all the key requirements are listed on the form, locate the best-known software suppliers that provide the type of functionality required. Suppliers can be found in many ways: through advertisements, recommendations from colleagues, information from professional organizations, the Internet, trade journals, and many other sources. Once the list is constructed, contact each supplier by phone or e-mail and see whether they claim to have a solution that meets your key requirements. If the response is yes, obtain rough costing information in an effort to determine total cost that includes the following:

- License fees
- Maintenance fees (upgrades and limited amounts of technical support, which typically run 15 percent to 20 percent of the license fee)
- Hardware cost (if required)
- Consulting costs (if required)
- Training costs (if required)

In addition, ascertain the following:

- How long has the supplier been in business?
- Has the supplier worked on similar installations? How many?
- Can the supplier provide at least three references?

With this information, the BPI team can hone in on suppliers they would like to take to the next level, which involves getting written responses to the questions on the Software Key Requirements Form. Place the names of these suppliers on your master copy of the Software Key Requirements Form. (See Figure 4-2.)

Page 1 of 2	**SOFTWARE KEY REQUIREMENTS FORM**			Date: 11/16/09
Required Function: Process Home Mortgage Loans				
	Key Requirements	**Suppliers**		
		ABC	**Gem Star**	**Great Ware**
1	Can your software integrate with the attached list of software and hardware?			
2	Does the package have a prequalification calculator?			
3	Does your package print & download standard forms (e.g., 1003, etc.) and data?			
4	Does your package have automated underwriting capability?			
5	Does the package have more than 25 status fields for tracking?			
6	Does your package have document exception reporting?			
7	Does your package have in-process exception reporting?			

Figure 4-2. Suppliers Selected to Respond in Writing

Step Three: Contact Each Potential Supplier

Contact the potential suppliers and inform them that you will be sending them a Software Key Requirements Form and that you want them to answer each question on the form with a "yes" or "no." In addition, specify that the supplier must support each answer with an attachment that elaborates on the correlation between requirements and product capability. As each response is received and reviewed, the team will indicate with a "yes" or "no" on the master copy of the Software Key Requirements Form if the product appears to meet the needs of each requirement. (See Figure 4-3.)

Page 1 of 2 — **SOFTWARE KEY REQUIREMENTS FORM** — Date: 11/16/09

Required Function: Process Home Mortgage Loans

	Key Requirements	Suppliers		
		ABC	Gem Star	Great Ware
1	Can your software integrate with the attached list of software and hardware?	No	Yes	Yes
2	Does the package have a prequalification calculator?	Yes	Yes	Yes
3	Does your package print & download standard forms (e.g., 1003, etc.) and data?	Yes	Yes	Yes
4	Does your package have automated underwriting capability?	Yes	Yes	Yes
5	Does the package have more than 25 status fields for tracking?	No	Yes	Yes
6	Does your package have document exception reporting?	Yes	Yes	Yes
7	Does your package have in-process exception reporting?	Yes	Yes	Yes

Figure 4-3. Master Copy of Software Key Requirements Form

Step Four: View Product Demonstrations

Once the information in Step Three has been received, evaluated, and posted on the master copy, the BPI team will select which suppliers to bring in for a product demonstration. The suppliers must understand that you want the key requirements demonstrated. Do not accept anything other than the demonstration of the key requirements. (Too often, the product being demonstrated does not possess the appropriate capabilities that were claimed.) Any potential supplier that fails to demonstrate the key requirements should be scratched off the list.

During or shortly after the demonstration, the BPI team will rate the product with respect to each key requirement, using a 0 to 5 rating. (See Figure 4-4.) A rating of 5 indicates that the software fully meets the specified needs; a rating of 0 means that the product does not meet the key requirement at all or was not available for review. Another thing to watch for during the demonstration is whether the software adds unwanted non-value-added activities to the process. This is all too often a by-product of bolt-on packages.

Page 1 of 2	SOFTWARE KEY REQUIREMENTS FORM			Date: 11/16/09
Required Function: Process Home Mortgage Loans				
	Key Requirements	**Suppliers**		
		Gem Star	**Great Ware**	
1	Can your software integrate with the attached list of software and hardware?	5	5	
2	Does the package have a prequalification calculator?	5	5	
3	Does your package download standard forms (e.g., 1003, etc.) and data?	5	4	
4	Does your package have automated underwriting capability?	5	5	
5	Does the package have more than 25 status fields for tracking?	5	5	
6	Does your package have document exception reporting?	5	5	
7	Does your package have in-process exception reporting?	5	3	

Figure 4-4. Rating Demonstrated Software

Step Five: Select the Bolt-On

After product demonstrations have been completed, the BPI team has enough information to select the bolt-on. The BPI team in this example agreed it would move forward with Gem Star, pending a reference check and executive approval, since it was the only supplier that fully met the key requirements, some questions posed during the reference check follow:

- Did the software require training from the supplier, and was that training adequate?
- In practice, how good is the documentation?
- How well did the supplier respond to any request for assistance?
- Were any bugs detected? How fast did the supplier react in correcting the bugs?
- Would you recommend the supplier?

Once the BPI team receives feedback on these and similar questions and obtains a formal written quote, it has enough information to perform a cost-benefit analysis and get executive approval (assuming the total cost was within expectation and responses on the reference checks were positive).

Additional Key Points

- It is not unusual that the demonstrated packages do not meet all of your key requirements. When this occurs, your choices are as follows:
  - Continue searching for a package that meets all your key requirements.
  - Determine whether you can do without the key requirement(s) that are missing.
  - See whether the supplier would be willing to modify its offering to accommodate your requirements.
  - Design and program your own solution (custom routine).
  - Apply the software "as is" and augment it with a custom routine.
- Anyone who has ever shopped for software understands that a rough cut of the available software offerings is necessary prior to bringing in a product for a demonstration. This rough cut is based on software capabilities required to perform the required activities, integration with the current system, and costs. A rough cut can be done by phone (or e-mail to save time), although most software suppliers are reluctant to answer questions on the phone and would rather secure a live appointment to "sell" their product. Insist on acquiring the information over the phone or by e-mail; otherwise, you risk inviting an endless parade of demonstrators trying to sell their products with capabilities that do not meet your needs and or with price tags management will never approve.
- From an implementation standpoint, the five steps discussed in this chapter are placed on the implementation milestone chart along with the following: write test procedures, perform test, write user operating procedures, train, and implement.

The Extension System Enhancement Option

5

An *extension* is the enhancement of an existing software module. It can be accomplished by 1) copying an existing module and then modifying it to meet your specific needs, or 2) adding a routine that is attached to a specific hook in the module, if available. Both approaches are covered and demonstrated in this chapter.

Copy and Modify an Existing Module

This is considered a viable option if the existing application can be modified to perform the required activities as defined by the business process improvement (BPI) team. The prerequisite is that the source code of the existing module is available. To modify an existing module:

1. Make a copy of the specific module that is to be modified.
2. Modify, as required.
3. Change the main procedure to recognize the copied/modified module.

Design the Modifications

The Extension Worksheet is used to reflect how the module will be modified. (See Figure 5-1.) Begin by filling out the worksheet header with the following information:

- Current date
- Name of team leader
- Names of team members
- Page number
- Task name
- Process name
- Hook name, if applicable (not applicable in this example)
- Name of the module being modified, if applicable (this is applicable in this example)

EXTENSION WORKSHEET

Date	**Team Leader**	**Team Members**	
06/15/2009	Phil Martinez	Jennifer Stewart, Jody Parker, Sam Baker, and Josh Martin	**Page 1 of 2**

Task Name: Customer Interface (*Name the task*)

Process Name: Order Entry (*Name the process*)

Hook: N/A (*Indicate hook name if applicable*)

Module Modification: Order Entry Module (*Module name to copy & modify*)

(Simply state, one operation at a time, the sequence in which the module will perform the operation, demonstrate as required, and note the modifications.)

1. The order entry module screen will be **modified** to reflect four command buttons at the bottom of the sales order screen as reflected below.

■ Enter Pricing ■ Availability Inquiry ■ Enter Order ■ Cancel Request

2. When a customer call is received by the customer service department the customer number will be entered into the order entry module. The order entry module will be **modified** to automatically populate the sales order header (e.g., customer name, address, address, terms, etc.) using the existing customer file that is in the system.

3. The customer service representative will then key in the quantities and part numbers requested by the customer. The order entry module will then be **modified** to automatically enter in the customer pricing on the existing sales order form once the "**Enter Pricing**" command button is engaged. It will then extend the amount per line item and enter a total for the bottom of the sales order.

4. If the customer is interested in delivery information prior to placing the order, the order entry module will be **modified** so that the customer service representative will then just hit the "**Availability Inquiry**" command button. This will initiate a check of the desired part numbers and quantities required against "available inventory" (e.g., unallocated inventory) and will automatically pop up the results on a small window on the far side of the order form. If the inventory is not available, the system will automatically determine the promised ship date based upon the lead time of the item, using the lead time in the system and manufacturing calendar as shown below, which also reflects the **pop-up screen design**.

Date: 6/15/2009

Part Number	Description	Quantity Required	Quantity Available	Lead Time	Promise Ship
154536	Rotor Mount	8	8		6/15/2009
156787	Shaft Mount	6	2	3 Days	6/18/2009

Figure 5-1. Extension: Copy and Modify Module Example

The three basic steps used to design the modifications are discussed below. To explain the steps and show what they can accomplish, the discussion is structured around a hypothetical company that has decided to modify one of its software modules to make entering sales orders less tedious and time consuming. What should become apparent as the discussion evolves is that manual activities can be significantly reduced by applying an extension, as demonstrated in the following example.

Example: XYZ Company is a heavy construction equipment manufacturer that has been in business forty years; a large segment of its business is part-replacement sales. It has a division that is solely responsible for the sale of replacement parts, and all customers in the database are repeat customers originating from the initial sale of the equipment. Its customer service department currently has twenty-five sales representatives, and they are 100 percent devoted to taking phone orders from customers. The orders, on average, take twenty minutes to complete, partly because the reps have to go through multiple screens to find information, such as customer bill-to and ship-to addresses, terms and conditions per their contracts, and availability of items in stock. Once the information is found, they have to enter everything by hand to create the sales order. When the sales order is created, two full-time inventory specialists enter into the system all the part number allocations (reserving on-hand inventory for each of the sales orders). The company decided to streamline the operation and created a BPI team. An Extension Worksheet was used to document the agreed-upon modifications to the current order entry module, and the steps below illustrate how the necessary modifications were made.

Step One: State the Sequence and Demonstrate

Simply state, one operation at a time, the sequence in which the module will perform the operation, demonstrate as required, and note the modifications. (See Figures 5-1 and 5-2.)

Step Two: Design the Input and Output Screens

Design the user's *input screen* (if required), which is the information the program needs from the user to initiate the program. Also design the user's *output screen* (if required), which reflects the results of the program's activity and reports. At Company XYZ, the modification to the order entry screen was reflected in the write-up under step one as well as the design of the pop-up screen. There was no need to repeat. (See Figures 5-1 and 5-2.)

Step Three: Determine New Data Requirements

Determine any new data requirements, if they are available and if they are accurate.The last step is reflected in Figure 5-2, where it was determined that no additional data was required to support the modification and the data required was accurate.

EXTENSION WORKSHEET

Date 06/15/2009	**Team Leader** Phil Martinez	**Team Members** Jennifer Stewart, Jody Parker, Sam Baker, and Josh Martin	**Page 2 of 2**
Task Name: Customer Interface (*Name the task*)		Process Name: Order Entry (*Name the process*)	
Hook: N/A (*Indicate hook name if applicable*)		Module Modification: Order Entry Module (*Module name to copy & modify*)	

(Simply state, one operation at a time, the sequence in which the module will perform the operation, demonstrate as required, and note the modifications.)

5. If the customer decides to:
   a. Place the order: The customer service representative will verify the order with the customer, and then hit the "**Enter Order**" command button. The sales order will then be placed into system and be **modified** to automatically create an allocation against the available inventory for the new sales order quantities.
   b. Not place the order: The customer service representative will hit the "**Cancel Request**" command button, which will eliminate the sales order form that was being created.

(Design the user's input screen, output screen, and reports, as required)

Modification to order entry screen already reflected and demonstrated. New pop-up screen already shown and demonstrated.

(Determine any new data requirements, if available, and if accurate.)

All data available in system and accurate. No additional fields need to be created.

Figure 5-2. Extension: Copy and Modify Module Example, *continued*

Apply a Routine to a Hook

A number of packages do not give access to the source code. Some programs, however, provide *routine hooks* that allow the user to insert customized programming onto the existing module that may then be used to perform the required activities. Hooks are typically provided for a specific purpose and the documentation typically indicates whether they are available.

Design a Routine for the Hook

The Extension Worksheet is used to design the routine that will employ the hook. (See Figure 5-3.) First, fill out the header of the worksheet with the following information:

- Current date
- Name of team leader
- Names of team members
- Page number
- Task name
- Process name
- Hook name, if applicable (it is applicable in the forthcoming example)
- Name of the module being modified, if applicable (not applicable in this example)

There are three basic steps used to design the modifications, as reflected in the following sections. As in the previous section, a hypothetical company will be used to illustrate how this works.

Example: Company ABC manufactures air purifier units; however, the company does not retain finish goods on the shelf. When a sales order is booked, the materials specialist creates a work order to build the booked items. For various reasons, the work order specialist to the manufacturing area may inadvertently fail to launch a work order to the floor, essentially making the sales order delinquent. The BPI team wanted to automate this process and found that a hook exists on the order entry module. The team used an Extension Worksheet to communicate the routine it wanted to apply to a hook to eliminate any further issues. (See Figure 5-3.)

Step One: State the Sequence and Demonstrate

Simply state, one operation at a time, the sequence in which the module will perform the operation, demonstrate as required, and note the modifications.

Step Two: Design the Input and Output Screens

Design the user's input screen (if required), which is the information the program needs from the user to initiate the program. Also design the user's output screen (if required), which reflects the results of the program's activity and reports.

EXTENSION WORKSHEET

Date 12/01/2008	**Team Leader** Phil Martinez	**Team Members** Jennifer Stewart, Jody Parker, Sam Baker, and Josh Martin	Page 1 of 1

Task Name: Automatically Create Work Order (*Name the task*) | Process Name: Shopfloor Scheduling (*Name the process*)

Hook: Order Entry Hook (*Indicate hook name if applicable*) | Module Modification: N/A (*Module name to copy & modify*)

(Simply state, one operation at a time, the sequence in which the routine will perform the operation, and demonstrate as required.)

Apply the following routine to the order entry module hook.

1. When a sales order is booked and saved, automatically assign a work order number to each item for the respective quantities booked.

Example:
Sales order number 16786 is booked and saved. The sales order has two items on it, as shown below.

(25) 56756 Toggle Ship Date 12/12/2008

(15) 65467 Toggle Sensor Ship Date 12/12/2008

The routine will automatically assign a work order number for the appropriate quantities as reflected below:

Example:

W078678 (25) 56756 Toggle

W078679 (15) 65467 Toggle Sensor

2. Have the routine automatically assign a due date for the work order that is one manufacturing day prior to the required ship date.

Example:

Due Dates Determined

W078678 (25) 56756 Toggle Due 12/11/2008

W078679 (15) 65467 Toggle Sensor Due 12/11/2008

Key Point: Manufacturing calendar is used to determine due date.

(Design the users input screen, output screen, and reports, as required)
Not required

(Determine any new data requirements, if available, and if accurate.)
All data available in system and accurate.

Figure 5-3. Extension: Apply Routine to Hook

At Company ABC, this step was not required. In such cases, the custom program attached to the hook will run in the background and will not require a user interface. The program execution will create a new work order in the existing work order module for the required products when a customer sales order is booked.

Step Three: Determine New Data Requirements

Determine any new data requirements, if they are available and if they are accurate. The custom program will use data from the existing sales order entry module to create a work order. At Company ABC, all the required data is available and accurate.

Additional Key Points

- Copying and modifying an existing module retains the ability to refer back to the original module if the need arises.
- It is important to ensure that whatever routine is being attached to the hook does not impact any other part of the system.
- From an implementation standpoint, the following are placed on the implementation milestone chart: design modification or hook routine employing the Extension Worksheet, program in-house, write test procedures, perform test and debug, write user's operating procedures, train, and implement.

The Supplier Modification Enhancement Option

6

If the user changes the source code of an existing software package, and then relies on service and upgrades from the supplier, trouble can ensue—in fact, the supplier can void the contracted support. Without question, the best time to understand that source code needs to change is *before* the package is purchased, for example, when searching for a bolt-on. When the business process improvement (BPI) team has determined the required activities—which are then stated in terms of key requirements (must-have functional capabilities of the software that will perform the required activities)—and has compared them with the product offering (as discussed in Chapter 4), that is the time to determine if the source code needs to change. When the supplier with the closest match is selected and the total cost of the product is within expectation, discuss with the supplier any gaps that exist between the key requirements and supplier's software capabilities. Find out whether the supplier is willing to make the required customization and support the modified package. Oftentimes, the supplier will accommodate the request for two reasons: 1) the desire to make a sale, and 2) the possibility that the modifications requested may be used for other customers. An additional incentive is that the fee charged will cover the supplier's development costs. Any gaps discussed with the supplier should be documented, along with the assurance that the supplier will support the package with upgrades and service.

Making Source Code Changes

As noted above, it is best to have the supplier make source code changes. The following approach to negotiating with the supplier is recommended:

- Determine the gaps between the standard package (whether it is an existing package or one being considered for purchase) and your key requirements.
- Determine whether the supplier is willing to modify the package. If so, the BPI team will spec out the exact modifications sought, generate a Supplier Modification Worksheet (specifying precisely which modifications are required), and present it to the supplier for review. Except for the heading (Supplier Modification Worksheet), this worksheet is nearly identical to the Extension Worksheet shown in Chapter 5.

- Follow up. Find out whether the supplier is willing to customize the product to your specs, how soon the required changes can be made, and how much the modifications will cost. Typically, when a supplier agrees to product modifications, the agreement includes ongoing support. However, this should not be assumed, and the software supplier must state in writing that software support will remain part of the deal. Make certain the cost of support is included in your discussions about modification.

These activities will dictate whether this is a viable system enhancement option for the specific project being worked on. Also be aware that top-level management may not always appreciate the technical aspects of customization, especially when procuring new systems. Be prepared to explain the need for the customization, preferably focusing on the benefits and anticipated impact if the modifications do not take place, as opposed to engaging in a technical discussion.

Source Code Change Example

A manufacturer of custom sheet metal products was procuring an ERP package, and the materials manager was well aware that the standard off-the-shelf package could not be used "as is" to drive the manufacturing floor. One of the main reasons this package was being purchased was to improve on-time deliveries of product as the business grew well beyond the manual methodologies that were in place. The supplier's estimated costs for the required modification of this $450,000 ERP system was $30,000. The materials manager explained to the president and his staff why these changes were *technically* required. The president, who had a sales background, listened politely and then denied the request. The package was purchased "as is" and implemented without modification. The net result of the implementation was that the percentage of on-time deliveries declined—the new low was worse than any the company had previously experienced.

The problem was communication. The materials manager thought and spoke in technical terms and focused on technical ramifications. Had he emphasized that the modification would significantly improve on-time delivery and help the company meet strategic objectives, management may well have been convinced.

Additional Key Point

The implementation milestone chart should reflect the following agenda: design the desired modifications employing the Supplier Modification Worksheet; negotiate cost and delivery and solidify agreement; write test procedures; perform test; write user operating procedures; train; and implement.

The Custom Routine System Enhancement Option

7

Custom routines are the mainstay of administration automation. This enhancement is applied more than any other system enhancement option, as it permits a high degree of creativity, flexibility, capability, and competitive differentiation without (in most cases) modifying the source code. This enhancement is often applied to eliminate a specific impediment to creating a fully automated supply chain system tailored to meet the specific needs of the environment. The custom routine is designed by the business process improvement (BPI) team to perform the required activities that the team has defined.

Basic Guidelines

Designing a custom routine is straightforward and is performed by the BPI team following three basic guidelines discussed below.

Basic Guideline #1

The entire task can be automated if:

- It is a repetitive process.
- A description of the step-by-step process can be verbalized.
- Data is available.

Basic Guideline #2

The system to which you are adding routines will ideally have import and export capabilities. (Most packages have import/export capabilities.) If an import/export capability does not currently exist, it can often be programmed into the system.

Basic Guideline #3

Stay within source code to avert revision issues.

Staying within Source Code Example

Creating purchase orders: The current source code for ERP system XYZ requires the user to key a requisition into the system. The requisition is then approved by someone with authority and reaffirmed by the buyer. The requisition then becomes a purchase order. (See Figure 7-1.) For this example, the goal is to trigger a requirement automatically (based on consumption) and then have the system automatically generate a purchase order.

Figure 7-1. Current Source Code

Custom Routine Approach

Once an item is triggered, have the routine automatically:

- Create the requisition (as if it were typed into the system).
- Approve the requisition (as if it were typed into the system).
- Create the purchase order (as if it were typed into the system).

End result:

1) The capability to create purchase orders immediately is achieved, and 2) the source code integrity of the purchase order system remains intact.

Designing the Custom Routine

The Custom Design Worksheet is used to design the custom routine and the modification process follows three basic steps (outlined below). The worksheet header includes the following information.

- Current date
- Name of team leader
- Names of team members
- Page number
- Task name
- Process name

The three basic steps used to design a custom routine are discussed below. To explain the steps and show what they can accomplish, the discussion is structured around a hypothetical company that has decided to create an automated routine to create their sales forecast. What should become apparent as the discussion evolves is that employing custom routines can significantly reduce manual activities and impediments to speed and accuracy.

Example: The NYG Company manufactures medical instrumentation and offers over 350 finish goods items. The company manually creates a sales forecast, which requires a tremendous effort in acquiring historical sales information from the database, which is then manipulated through a series of hand calculations. The BPI team has identified the manual forecasting task as the root cause issue of material shortages due to not receiving the sales forecast in a timely manner for procurement purposes coupled with erroneous forecasts due to inaccurate hand calculations. The BPI team selected custom routine as the system enhancement option to alleviate these issues.

Step One:

State Each Operation, Determine the Sequence in Which the Program Will Perform the Operations, and Demonstrate (See Figure 7-2.)

As the figure shows, the BPI team has designed a program to Automatically Create a Forecast, which is a task that is used to support the Master Schedule Process. The Custom Routine Design Worksheet communicates to the programmer exactly how the program should operate. The worksheet explains the program one step at a time, beginning with the first step and continuing until all the steps have been covered. After each step is explained, it is demonstrated so that there is no guesswork about what is required.

Step Two:

Design the Input Screen (the Information the Program Needs from the User to Initiate the Program) and the Output Screen That Reflects the Results of the Programs Activity and Reports (See Figure 7-3.)

Step Three:

Determine the Custom Program Data Requirements

The last step is reflected in Figure 7-4, which determines the data that is required for the custom routine to function, if it is available and accurate.

Custom routines are designed in-house and are generally programmed in-house, but some companies find it necessary to outsource the programming when the internal capabilities do not exist or if the timeframe required for completion is too tight. If outside programming is necessary, the following steps are recommended:

1. First, clearly identify your software package.
2. Locate a supplier (use the guidelines related to bolt-on enhancement, presented in Chapter 4).
3. Create a clear Request for Quote and forward to the supplier with the Custom Routine Design Worksheet developed by the BPI team.
4. Be realistic about the expected completion date.
5. Assign one individual to be the contact point with the selected supplier.

CUSTOM ROUTINE DESIGN WORKSHEET

Date	Team Leader	Team Members	
10/1/2008	Tom Myers	Mike Sanders, Frank O'Neill, Bob Green, and Sandy Jean	Page 1 of 3

Task Name: Automatically Create Forecast (*Name the task*)	Process Name: Master Schedule (*Name the process*)

(Simply state, one operation at a time, the sequence in which the program will perform the operation, and demonstrate as required.)

1. The user will access the forecast routine and be prompted to input a "From Date" and "To Date." The user will also input a "Times Factor" for each month they want the program to generate a forecast starting with the current month. The user will then click on the "**Calculate**" button to engage the program.

User Input Example:

- Today's Date: 10/01/2008
- From Date = 9/01/2008……To Date = 9/30/2008
- .90 Times Factor October, 2008…., 1.1 Times Factor November, 2008…..

2. The program will begin by picking up the "Historical Sales" quantity that took place for each part number that is coded in the system as a Master Schedule item that took place during the "From Dates" to the "To Dates" that the user inputted. The quantities picked up for each part number will then be totaled by the program.

Program Calculation Example:

Master Schedule Part Number	Description	"From Date" "To Date" Histor. Sales	.90 Times Factor October 2008	Average Daily Demand October 2008	1.1 Times Factor November 2008	Average Daily Demand November 2008
5123	Monitor AC	1000				
5298	Monitor PG	1400				
5300	Monitor GH	800				

3. Next, the program will multiply each month's "Times Factor" times each of the part numbers "Historical Sales" to determine the anticipated sales level for each month that a "Times Factor" was inputted. Round up! See below.

Master Schedule Part Number	Description	"From Date" "To Date" Histor. Sales	.90 Times Factor October 2008	Average Daily Demand October 2008	1.1 Times Factor November 2008	Average Daily Demand November 2008
5123	Monitor AC	1000	900		1100	
5298	Monitor PG	1400	1260		1540	
5300	Monitor GH	800	720		880	

Figure 7-2. Each Step of The Custom Design is Verbalized and then Demonstrated

CUSTOM ROUTINE DESIGN WORKSHEET

Date	Team Leader	Team Members	
10/1/2008	Tom Myers	Mike Sanders, Frank O'Neill, Bob Green, and Sandy Jean	Page 2 of 3

Task Name: Automatically Create Forecast	Process Name: Master Schedule

4. Next, the program will divide the anticipated sales level for each part number (e.g., 5123) for each month (e.g., October) by the number of manufacturing days (e.g., 23 days in October) in the specific month to equal the Average Daily Demand (e.g., Part number 5123 – October = 900 units/23 Days = 39.1 rounded up to nearest whole number = 40). Number of Manufacturing Days in example October 23 Days, November 20 Days.

Program Calculation Example:

Master Schedule Part Number	Description	"From Date" "To Date" Histor. Sales	.90 Times Factor October 2008	Average Daily Demand October 2008	1.1 Times Factor November 2008	Average Daily Demand November 2008
5123	Monitor AC	1000	900	40	1100	55
5298	Monitor PG	1400	1260	55	1540	77
5300	Monitor GH	800	720	32	880	44

5. Once the program has calculated the "Average Daily Demand" for each part number, for each month, the user will review the average daily demand via screen and have override capability. Once the user has completed the review, the user will click on the "**Load Forecast**" button, which will automatically place the "Average Daily Demand" for each Master Schedule part number, for each manufacturing day of the month, in the master schedule "Gross Requirements" row. Example, for Master Schedule part number 5123 the program will load a quantity of 40 units in for each manufacturing day for the month of October, and then 55 units per day for the month of November.

(Design the users input screen, output screen, and reports, as required)

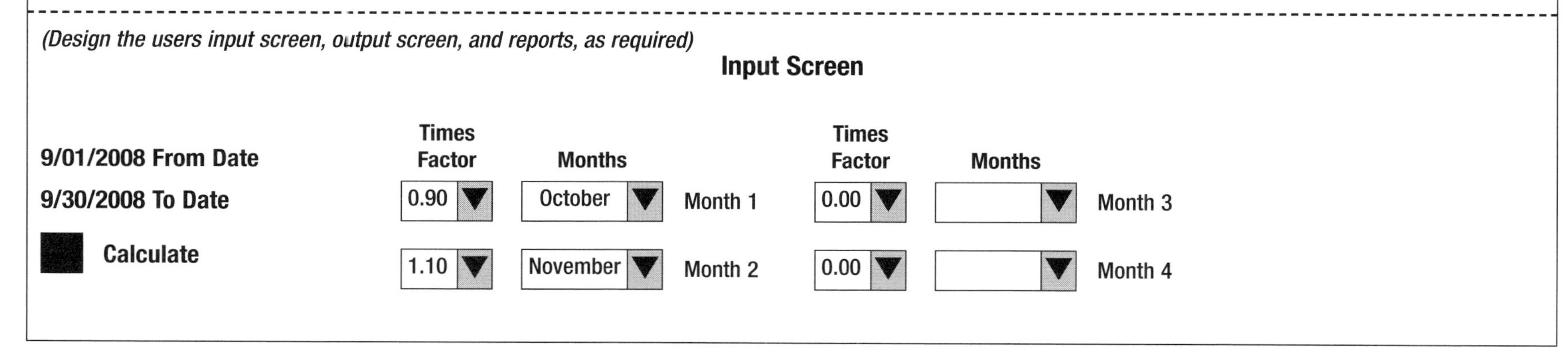

Figure 7-3. Input Screen, Output Screen, and Reports are Demonstrated as Required

CUSTOM ROUTINE DESIGN WORKSHEET

Date	Team Leader	Team Members	
10/1/2008	Tom Myers	Mike Sanders, Frank O'Neill, Bob Green, and Sandy Jean	Page 3 of 3

Task Name: Automatically Create Forecast | Process Name: Master Schedule

Output Screen

Load Forecast

Part		Historical Average Daily Demand			Projected Average Daily Demand			
Number	Description	Month 2	Month 1	Month 0	Month 1	Month 2	Month 3	Month 4
5123	Monitor AC	40	47	44	40	55	0	0
5298	Monitor PG	50	59	61	55	77	0	0
5300	Monitor GH	35	41	35	32	44	0	0

1. Place in part number sequence for all part numbers.
2. Want part number search capability.
3. Want report print capability.

(Determine the programs data requirements, if it is available, and if it is accurate.)

Data Required:

Part Number: OK **Description: OK** **Historical Sales by Day: OK, 2 years worth.** **Inventory Classification Code, OK**

——— END AUTOMATICALLY CREATE FORECAST ———

Figure 7-4. Determine Data Requirements and Determine Availability and Accuracy

6. Ensure the contract states that you own the source code.
7. Ensure the contract contains a warranty clause that bugs or other issues will be addressed and corrected by supplier.

Additional Key Points

- An IT representative should always be a part of your BPI team. This individual must have intimate knowledge of the system, have programming skills, and have participated from beginning to end in the project. The guidance and insight offered is invaluable.
- From an implementation standpoint, the following is placed on the implementation milestone chart: design program employing the Custom Routine Design Worksheet; write program test procedures; perform test and debug; write user operating procedures; train; and implement.

The System Enhancement Selection Process

8

The determination of which system enhancement option(s) to select is dependant upon a number of basic factors, including costs, required timing/urgency, in-house programming capabilities, and standard functional capability. Each of these basic factors must be taken into consideration during the selection process.

- **Costs:** Throughout the project, the BPI team leader updates the executive team. The executive team, in turn, provides the team leader with an approximate budget for the project, which is taken into consideration during the system enhancement selection process. For a selection to be considered cost effective, there would have to be a payback greater than the expenditures within a company-defined period of time.
- **Timing/urgency:** During the system enhancement selection process, the team must keep in mind its timeline for meeting the strategic objective(s). Often, more than one system enhancement option can provide the required capability, but only one satisfies time requirements. Sometimes, the degree of urgency and lead time in gaining the desired capability dictates the selection.
- **In-house programming capabilities:** Most companies have excellent programming capabilities, but this is not the case in certain environments. If there is no one on staff able (or available) to perform the required programming, a bolt-on or external programming may have to be considered.
- **Standard functional capability:** If a company requires certain standard functional capabilities, (such as Internet, EDI, and desktop faxing), these should be purchased.

Figure 8-1 provides an overview of the system enhancement selection process. Note that the process is illustrated as a flowchart with yes/no questions guiding the decision making. In most cases, the flowchart indicates that there is one "best" choice—the option that best satisfies the four basic factors listed at the beginning of this chapter.

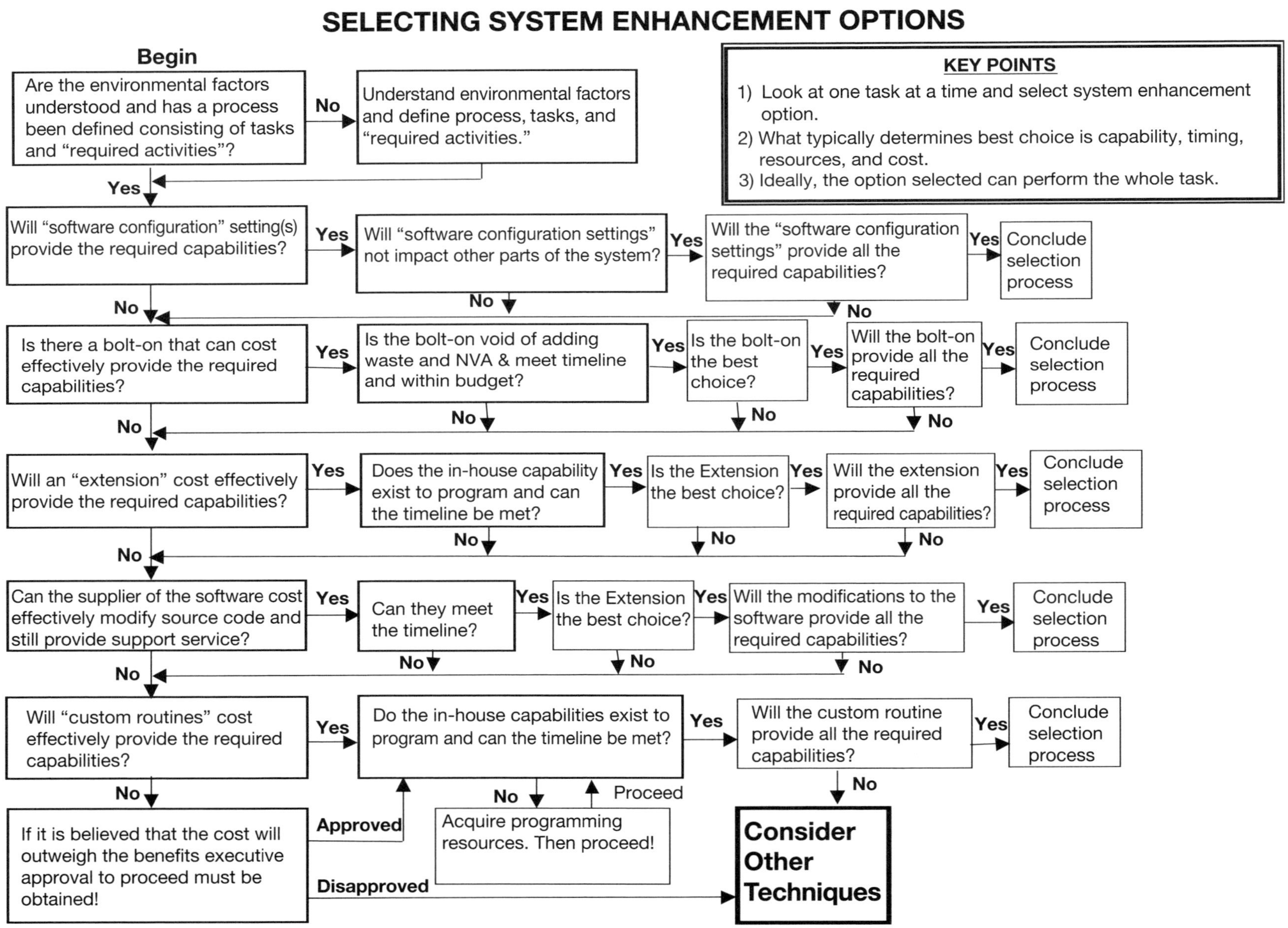

SELECTING SYSTEM ENHANCEMENT OPTIONS

KEY POINTS

1) Look at one task at a time and select system enhancement option.
2) What typically determines best choice is capability, timing, resources, and cost.
3) Ideally, the option selected can perform the whole task.

Begin

Are the environmental factors understood and has a process been defined consisting of tasks and "required activities"?
No
Understand environmental factors and define process, tasks, and "required activities."
Yes

Will "software configuration" setting(s) provide the required capabilities?
Yes
Will "software configuration settings" not impact other parts of the system?
Yes
Will the "software configuration settings" provide all the required capabilities?
Yes
Conclude selection process
No

Is there a bolt-on that can cost effectively provide the required capabilities?
Yes
Is the bolt-on void of adding waste and NVA & meet timeline and within budget?
Yes
Is the bolt-on the best choice?
Yes
Will the bolt-on provide all the required capabilities?
Yes
Conclude selection process
No

Will an "extension" cost effectively provide the required capabilities?
Yes
Does the in-house capability exist to program and can the timeline be met?
Yes
Is the Extension the best choice?
Yes
Will the extension provide all the required capabilities?
Yes
Conclude selection process
No

Can the supplier of the software cost effectively modify source code and still provide support service?
Yes
Can they meet the timeline?
Yes
Is the Extension the best choice?
Yes
Will the modifications to the software provide all the required capabilities?
Yes
Conclude selection process
No

Will "custom routines" cost effectively provide the required capabilities?
Yes
Do the in-house capabilities exist to program and can the timeline be met?
Yes
Will the custom routine provide all the required capabilities?
Yes
Conclude selection process
No
Acquire programming resources. Then proceed!
Proceed

If it is believed that the cost will outweigh the benefits executive approval to proceed must be obtained!
Approved
Disapproved

Consider Other Techniques

Figure 8-1. Selecting System Enhancement Options Guideline

Selecting the Best System Enhancement Option

To find the "best" choice, the BPI team must carefully review each of the system enhancement options. Keep the following in mind:

- The BPI team already knows its required activities, budget, timing, and in-house programming capability. A few phone calls to the right people can yield other preliminary information.
- Each system enhancement option selected tends to be a natural fit for specific conditions or situations. For example:
  - Choose a configuration setting if it can resolve a problem or issue identified by the BPI team, because it is already available.
  - Choose a bolt-on if it can perform the required activities without creating non-value-added activities, is within timeline and budget, and is cost effective.
  - Choose an extension if it requires a few lines of code and can be added to an existing hook, and if the programming capability exists in-house.
  - Choose an existing module if the source code is available, it can be copied and modified by in-house programmers, can stay within the timeline, and is cost effective.
  - Choose a software provider that is willing to change source code and support the package, within budget and timeline, and is cost effective.
  - Finally, understand that the custom routine is the mainstay of administration automation simply because of its high versatility; it can quite comfortably fill gaps other options cannot fill. It must, of course, be cost effective, but in the vast majority of cases, the costs are only a fraction of the benefits. As long as in-house programming capability exists and programming can be done within timeline, this is often the best selection if the other options do not fully satisfy the company's needs.

Encouraging Creativity and Innovation

There is no limit to the benefits that can be gained from developing highly effective processes that are then automated. Until this point in time, applying lean manufacturing to the office and/or the application of commercial off-the-shelf software were the only tools available in the hope of creating a competitive advantage. It is without question that improvement has been made in a number of companies applying these two other methodologies but the level of improvement typically does not qualify as being the absolute best in the world. These methodologies fall short as lean manufacturing techniques were designed for the shop floor and commercial off-the-shelf software is not tailored to meet the needs of the company thus becoming another "me too" contender. This text offers a methodology that is far superior and represents a clear, competitive advantage providing there is the desire to be the absolute best in the world coupled with the encouragement of the people to apply their creativity and innovation, which is necessary to compete in today's competitive climate.

Part Three of this book presents a strong and proven methodology for creating a truly lean office: the seven steps of administration automation. These seven steps open up a whole new frontier of lean and are an ideal choice for the company looking for an opportunity to transcend lean's current borders. Early adopters who take advantage of this opportunity can, in most cases, excel well beyond their competition.

Additional Key Point

IT has the main responsibility for ensuring that the enhancements selected by the BPI team do not impact any other area of the system, regardless of whether it is a configuration setting or custom routine. These lean office techniques, like any other technique or tool, must be fully understood before being applied.

PART THREE

Seven Steps of Administration Automation

The office is rich with opportunities to reduce costs, increase speed, and create differentiation from the competition while at the same time creating a multiplier effect that elevates the administration staff from performing mundane repetitious tasks to performing strategic-level activities. The lean office is designed to accomplish this goal by identifying office waste and non-value-added activities and by reducing processes to only required activities, which are then automated to the fullest extent possible. Equally important is that the lean office identifies and rectifies root cause issue(s) and creates a competitive advantage through innovation. An excellent and innovative methodology for creating a lean office is the *seven steps of administration automation*. This part of *Creating the Ultimate Lean Office* explains each of the seven steps and demonstrates each step with an ongoing example.

Note: The Seven Steps of Administration Automation Flow Chart is located in Chapter 3.

Step 1: Improvement Driven by Strategic Objectives

9

Companies develop strategies on how they will compete and the company is aligned to support its direction. There are many methods used to develop company strategy but at a minimum they are formulated after performing an external and internal analysis in an attempt to determine performance gaps or where competitive advantage may be achieved. Strategic objectives are then stated to the organization specifying what has to be accomplished by what point in time. The strategic objectives of a company dictate the type of processes that are put into place which in turn supports achieving the company strategy. There are times, however, when an executive mandate is given in Step 1 that is not derived from the formulation of strategy but rather in response to high-profile issues or concerns. The executive mandate is communicated in terms of strategic objective(s) and will not be discussed further as it is straightforward and follows the same sequence of steps from Step 2 forward.

External Analysis

An external analysis typically includes customers, competitors, economy, government regulations, and technology. This information is available from a multitude of sources and is gathered and assessed to understand the environment under which the company is operating. An external analysis is used to shape a company's strategy, which may lead to, as an example, new products and/or services; establishing or removing distribution centers; decisions related to costs, quality, and/or delivery; outsourcing, acquisitions; and so on. Before formulating a strategy, the company will also perform an internal analysis to determine its own strength and weaknesses in relation to external factors.

Perform Internal Analysis and Determine Gaps and/or How Competitive Advantage Can Be Achieved

After assessing the external environment, the company should determine its own strengths and weaknesses. It should employ the same criteria to evaluate its own position as what was deemed "vital to compete" from the external analysis findings. If gaps exist, create a "gap statement."

Determine a Strategy and State the Strategic Objective(s)

Based upon the external and internal analyses, the company now formulates its strategy. The strategy can be 1) reactive in response to external forces, 2) proactive in developing a competitive advantage, or 3) left unchanged.

Upper-level management will communicate exactly what must be accomplished, by what date, to achieve the strategy—that is, state the strategic objective(s). Strategic objective(s) unifies the company in a concentrated effort to accomplish what the company deems vital to its survival and/or growth. Consider the following example:

The company: Magnum Lock, Inc., manufactures replacement door locks. The outlet for its product is retailers.

Environmental factors:

- Customer demand for all products is linear.
- Magnum offers 570 products.
- Magnum can forecast sales dollars fairly accurately and therefore knows the percent of increase or decrease of anticipated sales levels.
- Product mix history within a reasonable margin of error repeats itself.
- Manufacturing lead time is two days for finished goods items; expectation for delivery among the major retailers, once order is placed, is five days (the five day lead time is consumed by Magnum's transportation time from the plant). The product, therefore, needs to be readily available on the shelf at Magnum in anticipation of orders being received.
- Magnum employs an MRP system in procuring and scheduling components. There are over 3,000 supporting part numbers.
- Component work cells are in place.

The issue: Magnum already knew it had an on-time delivery issue but became somewhat complacent after performing a competitive analysis of its major competitor (Lockland). The external analysis indicated that the competition (that is, the industry standard) was performing no better. However, since Magnum had been losing market share over the past six months, management decided to perform another external analysis, and the results were not good: Magnum's major competitor, Lockland, was now exceeding industry standards, and customers were favoring Lockland. Lockland's performance was as follows:

- Customer quoted lead time: five days
- Customer on-time delivery: 98 percent
- Inventory turn ratio: three
- Pricing: Comparable to Magnum
- Quality: Comparable to Magnum

Magnum then performed an internal analysis and determined its own performance level, which, when compared with Lockland's, revealed a significant gap in performance. Magnum's customer on-time delivery was 75 percent compared with Lockland's 98 percent. The company created a gap statement, shown in Figure 9-1.

GAP STATEMENT			
Lockland Performance		Magnum Performance	
Customer quoted lead time	5 days	Customer quoted lead time	5 days
Customer on-time delivery	98%	Customer on-time delivery	75%
Inventory turn ratio	3	Inventory turn ratio	3
Price comparison to Magnum	Comparable	Price comparison to Lockland	Comparable
Quality comparison to Magnum	Comparable	Quality comparison to Lockland	Comparable
Gap Statement: Lockland on-time delivery is 98%. Our on-time delivery is 75%.			

Figure 9-1. Gap Statement

The external analysis revealed that Magnum's primary competitor, Lockland, had made significant strides in improving its customer on-time delivery and was more attractive to retailers. This gave Magnum a clear and straightforward strategy: to meet or exceed Lockland's on-time delivery. Magnum then determined its strategic objective: "We will increase our customer on-time delivery from 75 percent to 99 percent or better by March 27, 2009."

Additional Key Points

- The number of strategic objectives for a company should be limited to two or three.
- The strategic objective(s) should be precisely stated and should include numerical values for the current position, the target, and the date for achieving the objective. Each strategic objective is communicated to the company.
- When strategic objective(s) are first identified, exactly how they will be accomplished may not be clear. These details will come later, after the teams are formed.
- Understand that the best of all processes are meaningless unless they are in alignment with the strategy of the company.
- If continuous improvement teams are used to drive improvement, they can very easily be working on the wrong processes. Example:
  - Magnum could be focusing on streamlining accounts payable versus improving customer on-time deliveries.
  - With everyone performing continuous improvement, the focus can also easily gravitate to improving tasks within a department as opposed to 1) looking at the whole process that transcends departmental boundaries, and 2) ensuring that the

intended result of the process is being met. With lean office, resources are committed to what the company deems to be the most crucial projects. These projects can involve shareholder strategy, company strategy, or operations strategy. This way there will be focus on key areas to improve.

Step 2: Selecting the Team and Putting Primary Measurements in Place

10

Chapter 9 addressed the first step of administration automation—analyzing external and internal conditions, determining gaps or areas where competitive advantage can be achieved, determining strategy, and formulating strategic objectives that will defend against a threat and/or create a competitive advantage. The equally important second step is selecting the people who will be responsible for achieving the strategic objective and establishing primary measurements prior to implementation to monitor the effectiveness of the new processes.

BPI Team Leader and Team Members

The team leader, selected by the executive staff, is someone who is highly respected, detail oriented, organized, skilled at leading people, and understands the company's products. The executive staff also designates an executive sponsor whose job is to oversee the project and provide support for the team leader. Working together, the team leader and executive sponsor select team members. The team should consist of the following:

- Subject matter experts: If the strategic objective deals with materials and manufacturing, then materials and manufacturing expertise is required. If it deals with product offerings, the team requires sales, marketing, and engineering expertise.
- An IT representative with programming capability who understands the current system intimately.
- People from other disciplines, as required, to gain a complete business perspective of the issue(s) and solution(s).
- A historian who:
  - is highly respected, has intimate knowledge of the company as a whole, has been with the company for many years,
  - knows the company's history and people; has product knowledge; understands customer buying patterns; and knows the quality of data in the computer;
  - can quickly point to those areas of concern that individuals with the technical expertise may not know about;

- often voices the opinions of other longtime, respected employees whose concerns must be addressed openly during the design process.

The success of the project increases proportionately to the level to which non-team members feel that their input was considered and appreciated. This is important since these people are often close to the situation and may be responsible for applying the new processes.

Ideally, the team can be devoted full time to the project. If not, the team must have regular scheduled meeting times, and all members must attend every meeting. In addition, the BPI team should have a dedicated meeting room, and all forms and charts should be hung on the walls of this room so that information concerning the project is readily available. (See Figure 10-1.)

We can continue with the Magnum Lock, Inc., example in the previous chapter, to demonstrate Step 2. In Step 1, the executive team determined Magnum's strategic objective: "We will increase our customer on-time delivery from 75 percent to 99 percent or better by March 27, 2009." It is apparent that this project will require the skill set of production, production planning, IT, and a historian.

Magnum executives selected the vice president of sales as the executive sponsor since he has an intimate knowledge of the company, had participated in the external analysis, and understood the importance of the project. The team leader, selected by the executive sponsor, once held the positions of production manager and materials manager, is well liked, and is a good leader. The selection of team members was based upon their functional roles within the company and their areas of expertise. The team consisted of the following:

- **Materials manager:** Although new to the company, she was an expert in various replenishment systems.
- **Production lead:** The production lead had been dealing with the existing situation for the last several years and knew the details of what was occurring.
- **Production planner:** The production planner knew the current production and material control system in detail.
- **Industrial engineer:** The industrial engineer had been with Magnum for 24 years and had served in many different positions based on the needs of the company. She was very knowledgeable about Magnum's products, customers, manufacturing processes, and materials system. She knew everyone in the plant, was highly respected, and was ideal for the role of team historian.
- **IT supervisor:** The IT supervisor had been with the company for many years, knew the current computer system intimately, and was also well versed in programming.

The team was well balanced from a functional and expertise standpoint and each member was qualified to contribute to the process of achieving the strategic objective.

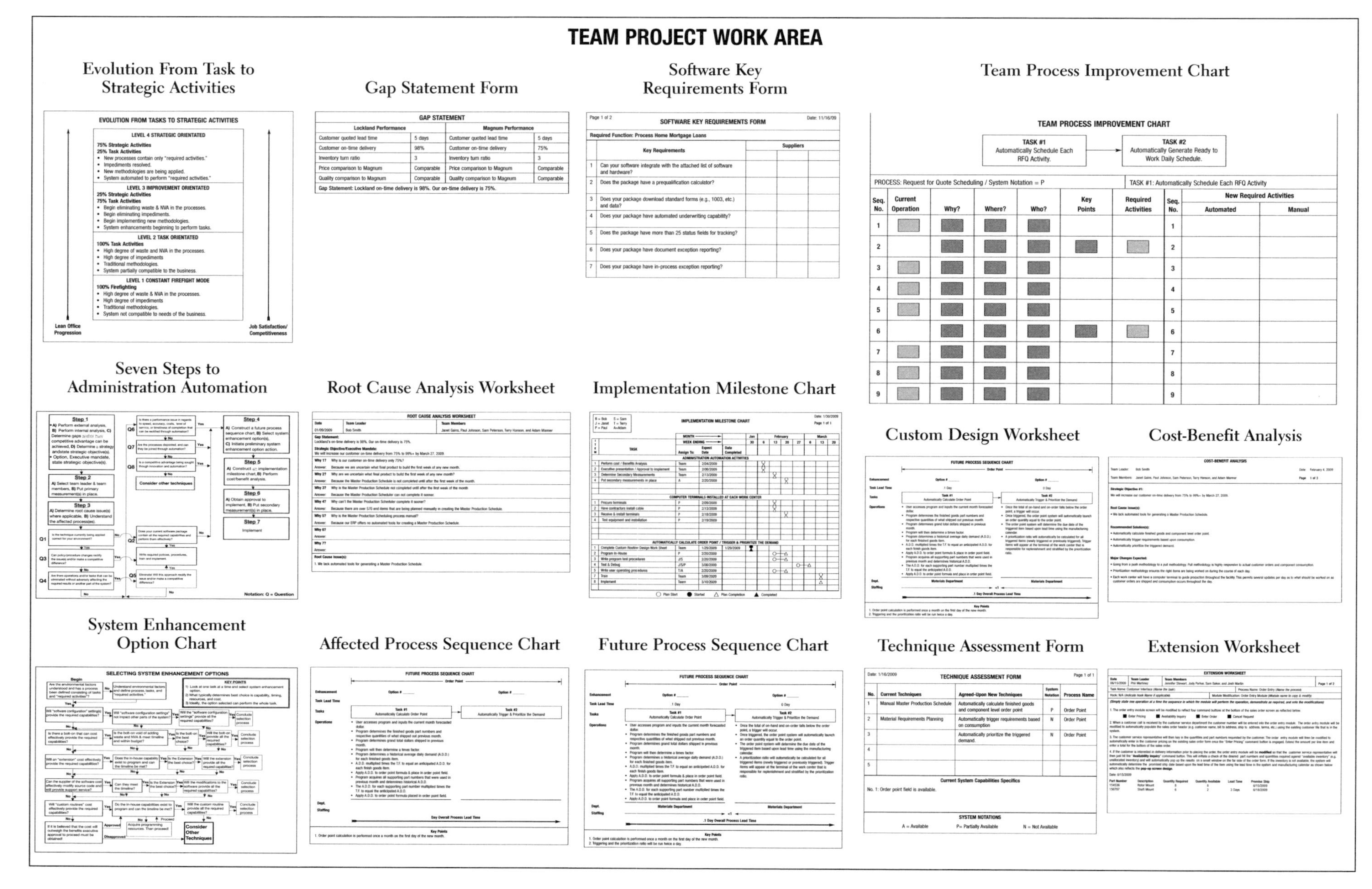

Figure 10-1. Team Project Work Area

Put Primary Measurements in Place

Once the team has been formed, the primary measurement(s) need to be put into place. The primary measurements are those that measure what the strategic objectives are focused on accomplishing. The primary measurement (generally displayed on a graph) should have a baseline, which might consist, for example, of a few weeks of data leading up to the project (that is based upon historical data); frequent updates are then posted at regular time intervals, to give visibility of performance level changes occurring (for example, weekly) after implementation of the new processes. Primary measurements flag the need for any adjustments that may need to take place (for example, increasing/decreasing the application of safety stock). The graph should also indicate the strategic objective goal. Accurate and ongoing measurement is a critical component of administration automation—it provides data (not opinion) to show progress toward achieving the strategic objective.

The Magnum team decided to use a Customer On-Time Delivery Chart, shown in Figure 10-2. The measurement was already automated and structured to give the customer on-time delivery in the time increment requested. The team decided to measure and chart performance weekly for reporting purposes. However, they planned to monitor the measurement daily immediately after implementation, permitting quick response to any issues.

Additional Key Point

Equally as important, a standard set of key operating statistics should always be in place with stated goals to ensure that the business as a whole is operating as desired. A set of charts or a dashboard needs to be made available and reviewed on a regular basis. There is a strong correlation between companies that find themselves in a constant reactionary mode to those who do not measure and monitor the well-being of their company on an on-going basis.

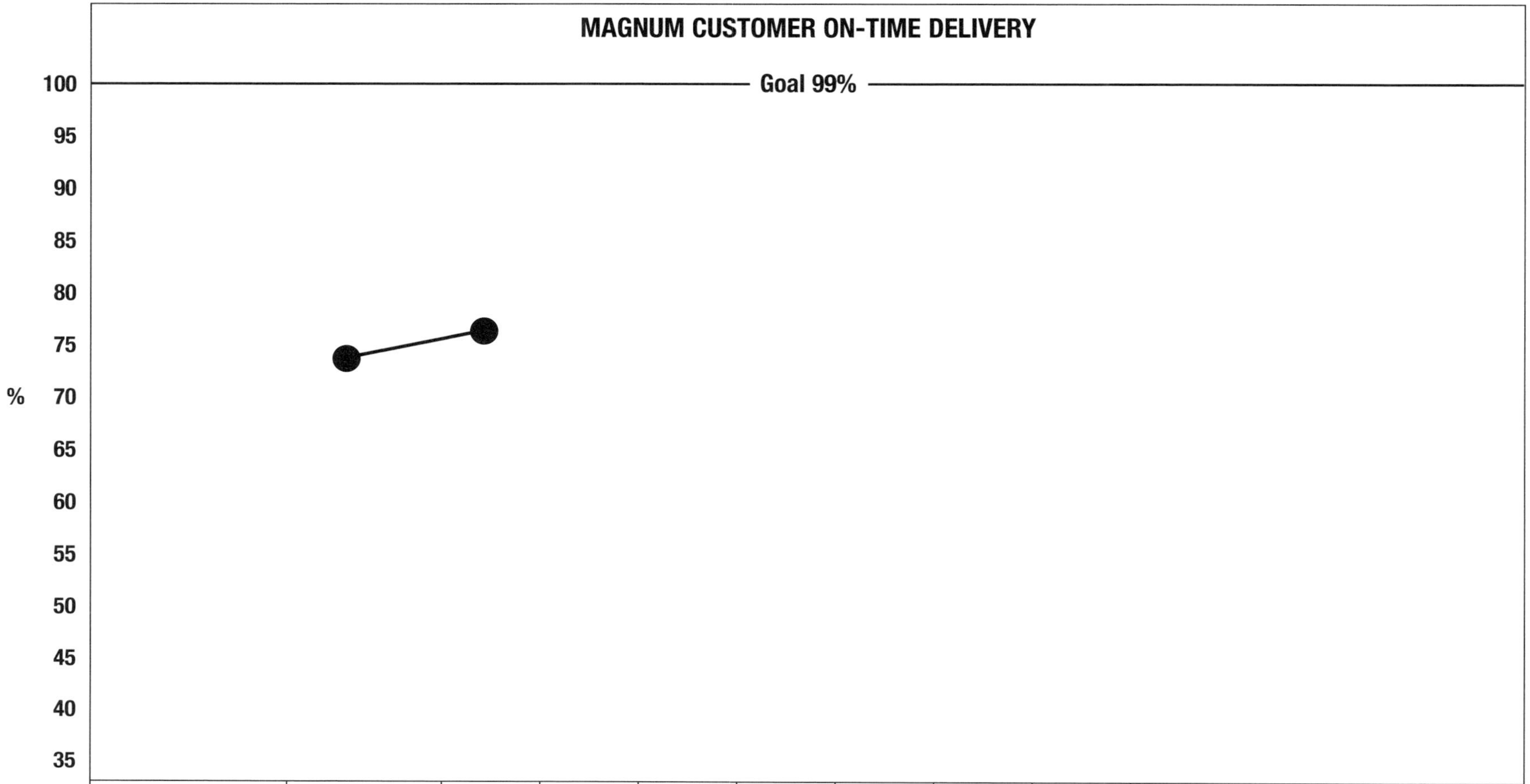

MAGNUM CUSTOMER ON-TIME DELIVERY

Goal 99%

%

100
95
90
85
80
75
70
65
60
55
50
45
40
35

Week Ending	Baseline	1/16	1/23	1/30	2/6	2/13	2/20	2/27	3/6	3/13	3/20	3/27
Qty Shipped	4,000	1,000										
Qty On-Time	3,000	780										
On-Time %	75%	78%										

Figure 10-2. Prime Measurement Put Into Place

Step 3: Determining Root Cause Issue(s) and Understanding Affected Process(es)

When Steps 1 and 2 are complete (external and internal analysis has been performed, gaps or areas where competitive advantage can be achieved determined, strategy determined, strategic objectives stated, team leader and team members selected, and primary measurements put into place), you are ready to determine the root cause issue(s) creating the gap(s), so that the affected processes can be identified, analyzed, and understood. We will cover the root cause analysis first, and then explain how to understand the current affected process(es).

Determine Root Cause Issue(s)

The most effective and straightforward approach to determine root cause issue(s) is simply asking "why" five times, because this method removes the layers of symptoms that disguise root cause issue(s). Although this approach is called the five whys, the number of whys you ask may be more or less, depending on how deep the root cause is. By discovering the root cause issue, the affected processes are identified. You can use a simple root cause issue worksheet for this purpose as shown in Figure 11-1.

The header information includes current date, team leader, and team members. The form should also include the gap statement, which is typically the difference between your company's performance and that of your competitors.

This clarifies the motivation behind the project and leads to the next point on the worksheet: the strategic objective specifying exactly what must be accomplished by when. Next, is the series of "why" questions, which you continue to ask until you reach the root cause issue. The root cause issue is entered in the box at the bottom of the Root Cause Analysis Worksheet.

If you were to use a Pareto chart to list all the root cause issues typically found in the office, the highest hitters would be 1) a high degree of manual activities creating excessive costs, lack of speed, timeliness issues, and errors, and 2) incorrect techniques being applied to the environment.

To illustrate this, we can return to the Magnum example used in Chapters 9 and 10. In Step 1, Magnum had determined and stated its strategic objective: "We will increase our

<table>
<tr><th colspan="3">ROOT CAUSE ANALYSIS WORKSHEET</th></tr>
<tr><td>Date</td><td>Team Leader</td><td>Team Members</td></tr>
<tr><td colspan="3">Gap Statement:

Strategic Objective/ Executive Mandate:</td></tr>
<tr><td colspan="3">Why 1?
Answer:</td></tr>
<tr><td colspan="3">Why 2?
Answer:</td></tr>
<tr><td colspan="3">Why 3?
Answer:</td></tr>
<tr><td colspan="3">Why 4?
Answer:</td></tr>
<tr><td colspan="3">Why 5?
Answer:</td></tr>
<tr><td colspan="3">Why 6?
Answer:</td></tr>
<tr><td colspan="3">Why 7?
Answer:</td></tr>
<tr><td colspan="3">Root Cause Issue(s):</td></tr>
</table>

Figure 11-1. Root Cause Analysis Worksheet

customer on-time delivery from 75% to 99%+ by March 25, 2009." Assume the current date is 01/09/2009. The objective at this point is to determine the root cause issue(s) which identify the processes that are of concern. These processes are *affected processes*, which will be examined to understand in detail what is occurring.

When the Magnum team applies the Root Cause Issue Worksheet, as reflected in Figure 11-2, it determines that the root cause issue is, "We lack automated tools for generating a Master Production Schedule."

The materials and manufacturing experts on the BPI team explain to the other team members that:

- The Master Production Schedule informs the final assembly line exactly what and how much to build based upon forecast and current customer orders and is also used to drive the Material Requirements Planning (MRP) module. Without a Master Production Schedule, the final assembly line is operating blindly, not knowing what to build to satisfy customer demand and creating customer order delinquencies.
- Because the MRP module is not being run until later in the month, precious time is also lost making the appropriate subassemblies and components needed to support the final production build.
- Customer orders do not always come in as forecasted and, ideally, the Master Production Schedule should not only be available on the first day of the month but also be updated frequently throughout the course of the month. It appears that the root cause analysis is accurate in identifying the root cause issue of why Magnum is experiencing only a 75 percent on-time record with its customers. The BPI team verifies its findings with the Master Production Scheduler and the Manufacturing Manager, who both concur with the root cause findings. The BPI team then proceeds to the next step.

Understand the Affected Process(es)

The tool used to understand the affected process is the Affected Process Sequence Chart, which reflects the current entire process. (See Figure 11-3.) It is used to understand the process in regards to the:

- Tasks and sequence of tasks that make up the process and associated lead time for each task
- Operations and sequence of operations that perform each task; it also indicates which operations are being manually performed by the manner in which it is written
- Which departments are performing the task to determine whether the process is disjointed
- Number of staff members who perform the task
- Overall lead time to perform the process

ROOT CAUSE ANALYSIS WORKSHEET		
Date	**Team Leader**	**Team Members**
01/09/2009	Bob Smith	Janet Gains, Paul Johnson, Sam Peterson, Terry Hanson, and Adam Manner
Gap Statement: Lockland's on-time delivery is 98%. Our on-time delivery is 75%. **Strategic Objective/Executive Mandate:** We will increase our customer on-time delivery from 75% to 99%+ by March 27, 2009.		
Why 1?	Why is our customer on-time delivery only 75%?	
Answer:	Because we are uncertain what final product to build the first week of any new month.	
Why 2?	Why are we uncertain what final product to build the first week of any new month?	
Answer:	Because the Master Production Schedule is not completed until after the first week of the month.	
Why 3?	Why is the Master Production Schedule not completed until after the first week of the month?	
Answer:	Because the Master Production Scheduler can not complete it sooner.	
Why 4?	Why can't the Master Production Scheduler complete it sooner?	
Answer:	Because there are over 570 end items that are being planned manually in creating the Master Production Schedule.	
Why 5?	Why is the Master Production Scheduling process manual?	
Answer:	Because our ERP offers no automated tools for creating a Master Production Schedule.	
Why 6?		
Answer:		
Why 7?		
Answer:		
Root Cause Issue(s): 1. We lack automated tools for generating a Master Production Schedule.		

Figure 11-2. Root Cause Analysis Worksheet Filled Out

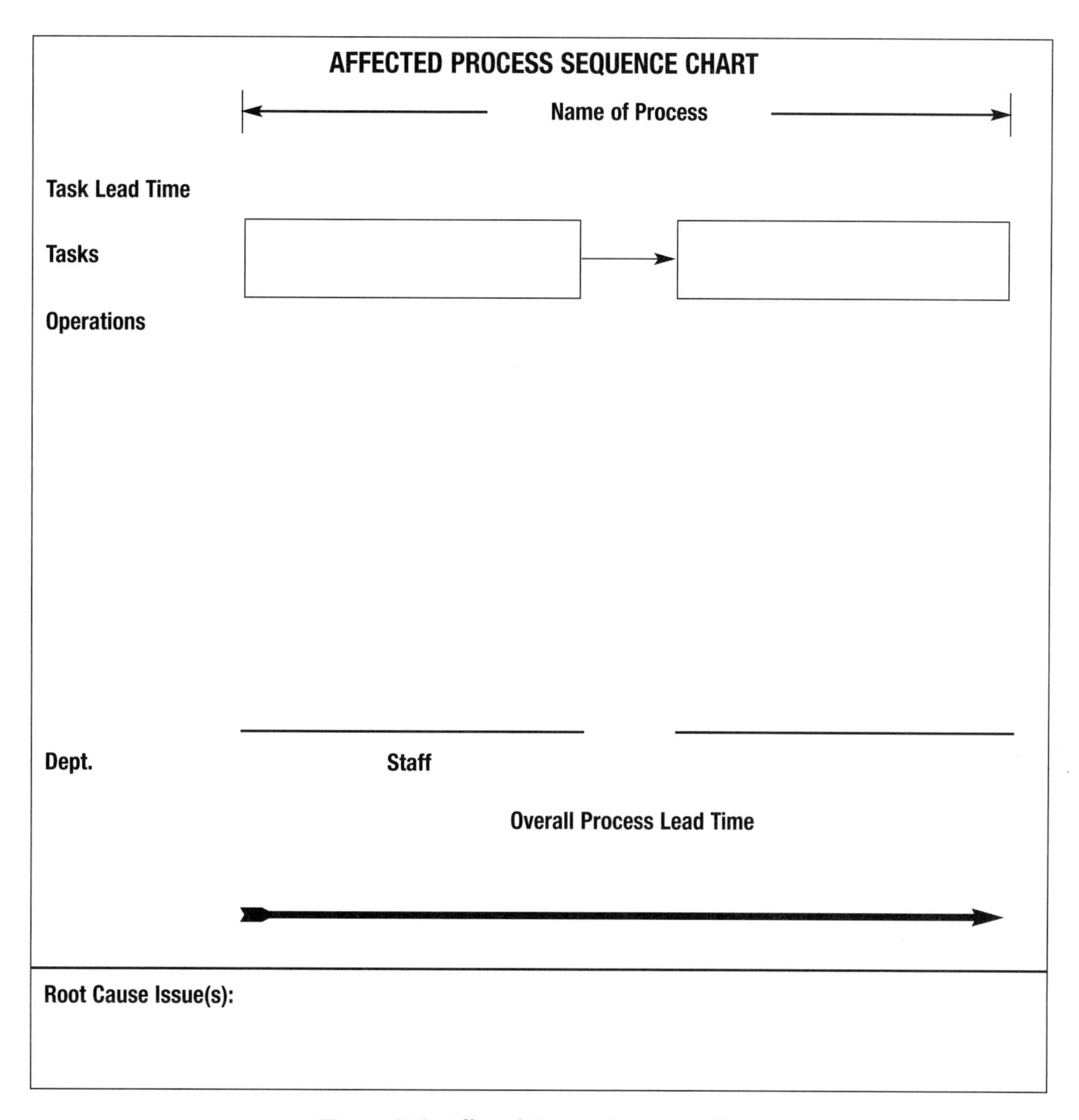

Figure 11-3. Affected Process Sequence Chart

The root cause issue that was determined earlier is indicated at the bottom of the Affected Process Sequence Chart to serve as a reminder of what to look for in the current process. The data collected on the Affected Process Sequence Chart will be used in Step 4 (see Chapter 13) to develop a Future Process Sequence Chart if the process is to be retained and reworked.

After identifying the root cause issue and the affected process, the Magnum BPI team works with the master scheduler in laying out the current master production schedule process using the affected process sequence chart. Figure 11-4 shows that:

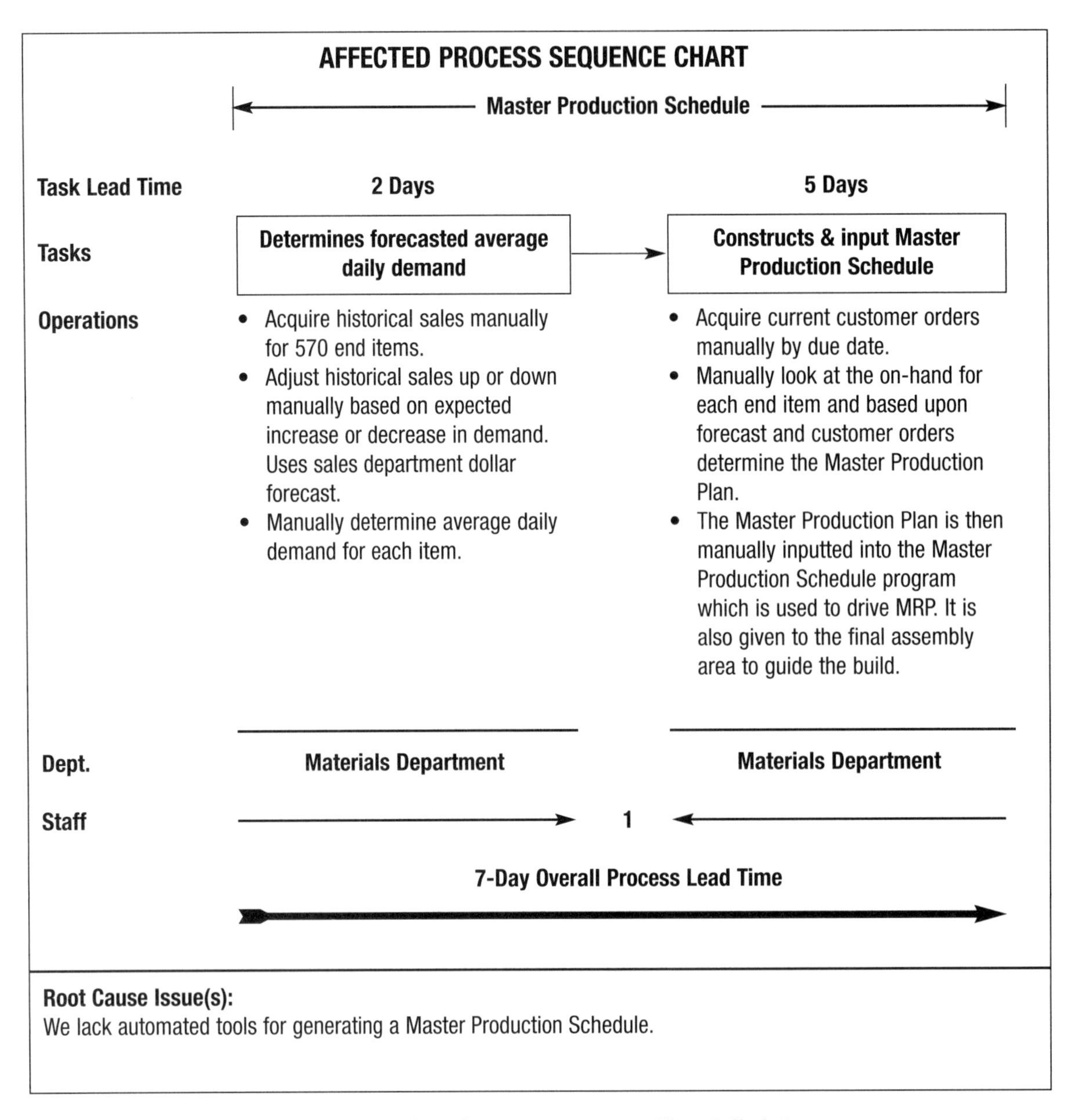

Figure 11-4. Affected Process Sequence Chart Filled Out

- It takes seven manufacturing days to develop the Master Production Schedule.
- Every operation is being manually performed.
- There is only one person performing this entire process.
- There is a lot of room for error in performing all these calculations manually.

After reviewing and discussing the data on the Affected Process Sequence Chart, the BPI team concludes that the Master Production Schedule is inaccurate the day it is issued! The reason? Reliance on forecast to determine what to build which was significantly aggravated by an extended period of time to produce the Master Production Schedule. Information is being picked up starting on Day 1 through Day 7, however, by the 8th day, when the Master Production Schedule is issued, new customer orders have been booked since Day 1, and that number can differ from what was forecasted. In addition, the Master Production Schedule comes out only once a month and continues to decline in accuracy as time goes on throughout the month due to the disparity between forecast and actual bookings. The manufacturing manager frequently has to reassess what is really required throughout the course of the month.

Additional Key Points

- The root cause analysis is an effective tool for identifying root cause issues and affected processes. It does not, however, inform the user if the technique that is being applied is correct for the environment. In other words, it points to the problem, not the solution.
- Additional team members can be added once the root cause issue is determined. In the example provided, the manufacturing manager and master scheduler may be added to the team if their ongoing contributions are required for the success of the project. Often, it is a good idea to include the people involved in the affected process so they can be part of the solution.

Eight Key Questions

12

After completing Step 3, you are now in a position to ask the eight key questions listed in the Seven Steps of Administration Automation Flowchart. (See Figure 3-2 in Chapter 3.) The purpose of these questions is to help determine if administration automation is an appropriate solution for the issue being addressed. Each of the eight questions is explained in this chapter.

Question 1: Is the Technique Currently Being Applied Correctly for Your Environment?

At this point, the BPI team has identified the root cause issue(s), understands the current affected process(es), and is in a position to evaluate whether the techniques currently employed are correct for the environment (for example, MRP versus kanban). This often entails an in-depth discussion.

If the Answer Is No

The team will determine the appropriate technique and fill out the Technique Assessment Form in Figure 12-1, completing the Current Technique(s), Agreed-Upon New Technique(s), and the Process Name of the new technique(s) columns. If more than one technique is involved, enter all of them and proceed to Question 2.

If the Answer Is Yes

Do not fill out the Technique Assessment Form. Skip Question 2 and go to Question 3.

Question 2: Does Your Current Software Package Contain All the Required Capabilities and Perform Them Effectively?

The BPI team needs to determine whether the system in place can effectively perform all the agreed-upon new techniques.

Date: ________	TECHNIQUE ASSESSMENT FORM			Page __ of __
No.	Current Techniques	Agreed-Upon New Techniques	System Notation	Process Name
1				
2				
3				
4				
5				
Current System Capabilities Specifics				
SYSTEM NOTATIONS				
A = Available	P= Partially Available	N = Not Available		

Figure 12-1. Technique Assessment Form

If the Answer Is Yes

Write the required policies and procedures, train, and implement. There is no need to go any further with the administration automation process.

If the Answer Is No

Document the current capabilities of the current system that pertain to the new techniques. Fill out the System Notation column next to each agreed-upon new technique on the Technique Assessment Form (see Figure 12-2), using A (available), P (partially available), or N (not available) as indicated at the bottom of the form. This information will be used in Step 4. (See Chapter 13.)

If you noted "available" or "partially available" next to any of the agreed-upon techniques, fill out the Current System Capabilities Specifics section of the Technique Assessment Form, indicating the Item Number of the new technique and the specific corresponding capability (for example, calculation routine) in the current system. Then go to Step 4 (see Chapter 13), as this process may be a good candidate for administration automation.

Date: 1/16/2009	TECHNIQUE ASSESSMENT FORM			Page 1 of 1
No.	**Current Techniques**	**Agreed-Upon New Techniques**	**System Notation**	**Process Name**
1	Manual Master Production Schedule	Automatically calculate finish goods and component-level order point	P	Order Point
2	Material Requirements Planning	Automatically trigger requirements based on consumption	N	Order Point
3		Automatically prioritize the triggered demand.	N	Order Point
4				
5				
Current System Capabilities Specifics				
No. 1: Order point field is available.				
SYSTEM NOTATIONS				
A = Available	P= Partially Available	N = Not Available		

Figure 12-2. Technique Assessment Form Filled Out

Question 3: Can Policy/Procedure Changes Rectify the Issue(s) and/or Make a Competitive Difference?

A number of issues can be resolved without revamping and/or automating the process by simply putting into place the appropriate policies and procedures. On numerous occasions, the author has seen highly expensive off-the-shelf systems put into place as opposed to putting into place appropriate enforced policies and procedures.

If the Answer Is Yes

If policies and procedures can rectify the issue or make a competitive difference, write them, train, implement, and enforce. There is no need to go any further with the administration automation process.

If the Answer Is No

Go to Question 4.

Question 4: Are There Operations and/or Tasks That Can Be Eliminated without Adversely Affecting the Required Results or Another Part of the System?

At times, additional operations or tasks over the years are added to an existing process to compensate for a condition that no longer exists. These additional operations and tasks may be the cause of the current issue.

If the Answer Is Yes

Go to Question 5.

If the Answer Is No

Skip Question 5 and go to Question 6.

Question 5: Will This Approach Rectify the Issue(s) and/or Make a Competitive Difference?

If the Answer Is Yes

If operations and/or tasks can be eliminated and if eliminating them will rectify the issue or make a competitive difference (if that is being sought), remove them, as long as the removal does not impact any other area of the system. Then write the required policies and procedures, train, and implement. There is no need to go any further with the administration automation process.

If the Answer Is No

If eliminating the operations or tasks will not make a competitive difference or resolve the root cause issue(s) go to Question 6.

Question 6: Is There a Performance Issue with Speed, Accuracy, Costs, Level of Service, or Timeliness of Completion That Can Be Rectified through Automation?

If the Answer Is Yes

This may be a good candidate for administration automation. Go to Step 4. (See Chapter 13.)

If the Answer Is No

Go to Question 7.

Question 7: Are the Processes Disjointed and Can They Be Joined through Automation?

If the Answer Is Yes

This may be a good candidate for administration automation. Go to Step 4. (See Chapter 13.)

If the Answer Is No

Go to Question 8.

Question 8: Is a Competitive Advantage Being Sought through Innovation and Automation?

If the Answer Is Yes

This may be a good candidate for administration automation. Go to Step 4. (See Chapter 13.)

If the Answer Is No

Consider techniques other than administration automation. Administration automation is a candidate for application for rectifying root cause issues in regard to speed, accuracy, costs, level of service, timeliness of completion, and for joining disjointed processes. It is also used to create competitive differentiation through innovation. However, prior to its application, we want to ensure that the current technique that is being applied is correct for the environment and that all other considerations such as policy, procedures, and current system capabilities that are typically overlooked have been considered.

Applying the Key Questions: The Magnum Example

Recall that Chapter 11 explained how Magnum identified the root cause issue and filled out the Affected Process Sequence Chart to understand the process, and determined that the company's Master Production Schedule was inaccurate from the day it was issued. This was due to the reliance of forecast to determine what to build coupled with an extended period of time to manually produce the Master Production Schedule.

The BPI team then began to addresses Question 1 on the Seven Steps of Administration Automation Flow Chart: **Is the Technique Currently Being Applied Correct for Your Environment?** Most of the team members thought this was a straightforward question that could easily be answered. They were right; the only problem was that each team member had a different answer! This initiated the process intended by the question, which is to:

- Challenge the current technique.
- Consider different techniques.

- Explore different methods of performing the various techniques.
- Brainstorm to determine the best technique and the best method.

The following were key points brought up by the team during the review process:

- One BPI team member suggested that the current technique was correct (Master Production Schedule) and so was the identified root cause issue ("We lack automated tools in generating a Master Production Schedule.") In his view, the Master Production Schedule process should be automated and produced daily.
- Another team member believed the current technique was incorrect for the environment and proceeded to back up her statement with the following:
  - The Master Production Schedule will never be 100 percent accurate since it contains forecasts. Even if the Master Production Schedule is automated and produced and issued each day, it will still be inaccurate as it contains forecast.
  - The appropriate technique for this environment would be to have finish goods sitting on the shelf, equal in quantity to average daily demand times lead time plus safety stock (order point). When an order is booked and shipped, it can be subtracted from finish goods inventory, which initiates a replacement order to the final assembly line. This way we are building only what is consumed. We can automatically calculate the order point and automate the triggering of the requirement to the final assembly line.
  - We could put into place an automated prioritization ratio based upon what is on hand versus what the order point should be (for example, final assembly part number 1234 = 60 on hand/100 order point = 0.60 priority; final assembly part number 1343 = 80 on hand/100 order point = 0.80) so that all the items that are triggered and need to be built are given a priority ratio. The automated prioritization routine would stratify what needs to be built by the lowest priority ratio which is most likely to stockout.
  - If we drive the finish goods build by order point and prioritization ratio, we should also drive the supporting components by order point and prioritization ratio.
  - Our environment has linear customer demand, which is ideal for these techniques to be effective. In addition, our sales volume for all our products is high.
  - We should have computer terminals at each work center so that as customer orders are shipped, replenishment orders are immediately triggered and are displayed at the terminal responsible for the finish goods build. The build of the finish goods will consume supporting components, which will immediately trigger and display at the terminals of the work cell responsible for replenishment. The supporting work centers on the floor will know the correct part numbers, quantities, and priorities of what to build as the triggering of order point and prioritization ratio will be updated several times a day.

  - As a side benefit, we may be able to significantly reduce our inventory, as our current inventory turn ratio is three turns with the MRP system. Pull systems tend to significantly reduce inventory.
- A third BPI team member stated that the current technique was correct, but recommended adding six more people to the administration department to enable getting the Master Production Schedule out daily. The Master Production process would be balanced from a labor content standpoint and have a buffer of people to add if the work was not getting done on time. In addition, the desks could be placed next to each other like a work cell and the area could be organized with visual factory techniques.

After debating the merits of these varied views, the BPI team agreed that:

- Adding more people to the problem was not a solution
- It would be better to build to what is consumed than building to forecast.
- A different technique was required to achieve the strategic objective. This new technique would automate 1) the order point calculation for both finish goods and supporting components, 2) the triggering, and 3) the prioritization.
- Computer terminals would be installed at each work center.

The team leader wanted to make sure that everyone understood that the root cause analysis had identified the correct root cause ("we lack automated tools in generating a Master Production Schedule") issue. He noted however that the technique currently in use was not appropriate for the environment and pointed out that while automating the current technique would lead to improvement, there was no guarantee that this would be enough to satisfy the strategic objective. The main reason cited for this was the problem with inaccurate forecasts.

Although Magnum's order point system would utilize forecasts to determine the order point (application of times factor), its triggering mechanism would be highly responsive to shifts in demand throughout the course of each day. In addition, the automated prioritization routine would ensure that work would be scheduled according to need (prioritization ratio), not by forecast. The BPI team leader then recommended that the IT supervisor begin looking at the cost of procuring and installing terminals and that the materials manager determine the anticipated changes in inventory and prepare for a cost/benefit analysis, which would be performed soon.

The BPI team then addressed Question 2: Does Your Current Software Package Contain All the Required Capabilities and Perform Those Effectively? In their discussions related to Question 1, the team agreed that Magnum should implement the following new techniques:

- Automatically calculate finish goods and component-level order point.
- Automatically trigger requirements based upon consumption.
- Automatically prioritize the triggered demand.

The team listed these techniques on the Technique Assessment Form, and the IT supervisor investigated the current computer system to determine if it contained the required capabilities. The only relevant item he found was an Order Point Field (the system lacked the calculation routine) and placed his findings on the form under System Notation (Partially Available) and Current System Capabilities Specifics (Order point field is available). (See Figure 12-2.)

Because the existing software package clearly did not have all the required capabilities for the new techniques, the team skipped the remaining questions (as per the Seven Steps of Administration Automation Flowchart) and moved to Step 4 (see Chapter 13) to develop the new process employing the agreed upon techniques.

Additional Key Points

- There is often more than one way to resolve a root cause issue and it is important that each member of the team is given an opportunity to present his or her thoughts.
- Stating that a specific technique will not work must be backed with a technical explanation. Too often, preconceived ideas have no foundation and limit the creativity of the group.

Step 4: Developing the Solution 13

After completing Steps 1 through 3 and addressing the eight key questions presented in Chapter 12, your BPI team knows the root cause issues, understands the affected processes, and has determined the appropriate techniques for the environment to achieve the strategic objective(s). In Step 4, you design a Future Process Sequence Chart, select the system enhancement option(s), and initiate preliminary system enhancement option action.

Constructing a Future Process Sequence Chart

The Future Process Sequence Chart reflects the completed, agreed-upon new process. (See Figure 13-1.)

This chart includes the following information:

- Name of the process
- Enhancement option(s) that will be applied to perform each task
- Estimated lead time to perform each task
- Task(s)
- Required operations that will be performed to complete each task
- Department(s) that will perform each task
- Estimated number of people who perform the task
- Estimated overall lead time to perform the process

When filled out, this chart provides an overview of the future process that will dictate your approach to creating custom routine designs, extension designs, key software requirements, supplier source code modifications, and implementation milestones. It also explains the agreed-upon process to all concerned. The Future Process Sequence Chart is developed by the BPI team and is derived from the Team Process Improvement Chart, a 48″ × 36″ wall chart employed by the BPI team in its dedicated team room to develop the new process, one operation at a time, for each task. (See Figure 13-2.)

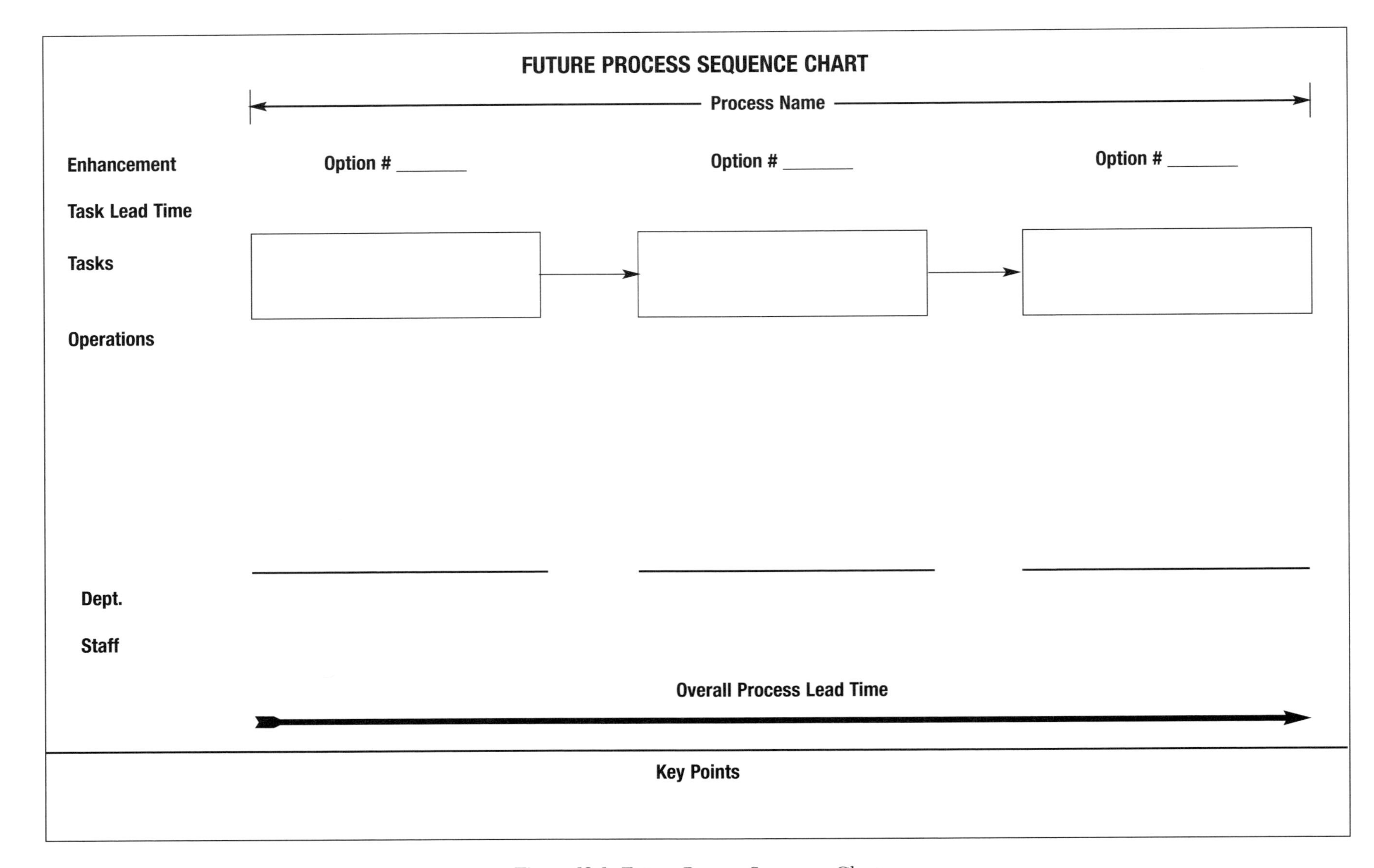

Figure 13-1. Future Process Sequence Chart

TEAM PROCESS IMPROVEMENT CHART

TASK #1 → TASK #2

PROCESS: ______________ / System Notation = __ | TASK # ______________

Seq. No.	Current Operation	Why?	Where?	Who?	Key Points	Required Activities	Seq. No.	New Required Activities	
								Automated	Manual
1							1		
2							2		
3							3		
4							4		
5							5		
6							6		
7							7		
8							8		
9							9		

Figure 13-2. Team Process Improvement Chart

Filling Out The Top Portion of the Team Process Improvement Chart

The team first fills in the name of the process that will be worked on and the highest system notation rating (A = Available is the highest rating, P = Partially available is the second highest, and N = Not available is the lowest) indicated on the Technique Assessment Form. The rating is based on assessment of the current software package and the current capabilities of the system to perform the desired process automatically, (see question 2 in Chapter 12), and shows if it is possible to make use of any current system capability while defining operations. The team then determines the basic tasks, in sequence, that need to be performed to complete the process. These numbered tasks are entered at the top of the chart with brief function descriptions (e.g., Task #1: Automatically schedule each RFQ activity; Task 2: Automatically generate ready to work daily schedule). Finally, the name of the task that the chart will be devoted to (e.g., Automatically schedule each RFQ activity) is placed on the chart.

Applying the Left-Hand Side of the Team Process Improvement Chart

If a process is to be retained but automated, enter the current task name and fill in the following information (see Figure 13-3):

- **Sequence Number:** This is the sequence in which the current operations are performed. The first operation is sequence 1.
- **Current Operation:** These are the operations currently performed; they are shown on the Affected Process Sequence Chart that was filled out in Step 3. For each current operation, fill out a 3″ × 3″ yellow sticky note with the name of the operation. Post the notes on the chart in the order they are performed, starting with the first operation at the sequence 1 row.
- **Why:** The next column shows why this specific operation was required and the information is derived from asking the five "whys." Write the final answer to "why" for each operation on a 3″ × 3″ light blue sticky note and attach to the chart. It is important to see whether any of the operations performed need to be retained (for example, complying with government regulations).
- **Where:** "Where" information comes from the Affected Process Sequence Chart and shows (by department) where an operation is performed. Write the information for each operation on a 3″ × 3″ light blue sticky note and attach to the chart.
- **Who:** Write the name of the person responsible for each operation on a 3″ × 3″ light blue sticky note and attach to the chart. This information is useful because the person working on a particular operation can often provide valuable insights about it.
- **Key Points:** The process of answering why, where, and who often brings to light key points that are important to consider while developing a new process. Write any key points on a blue sticky note and attach it under the key points column for the appropriate current operation.

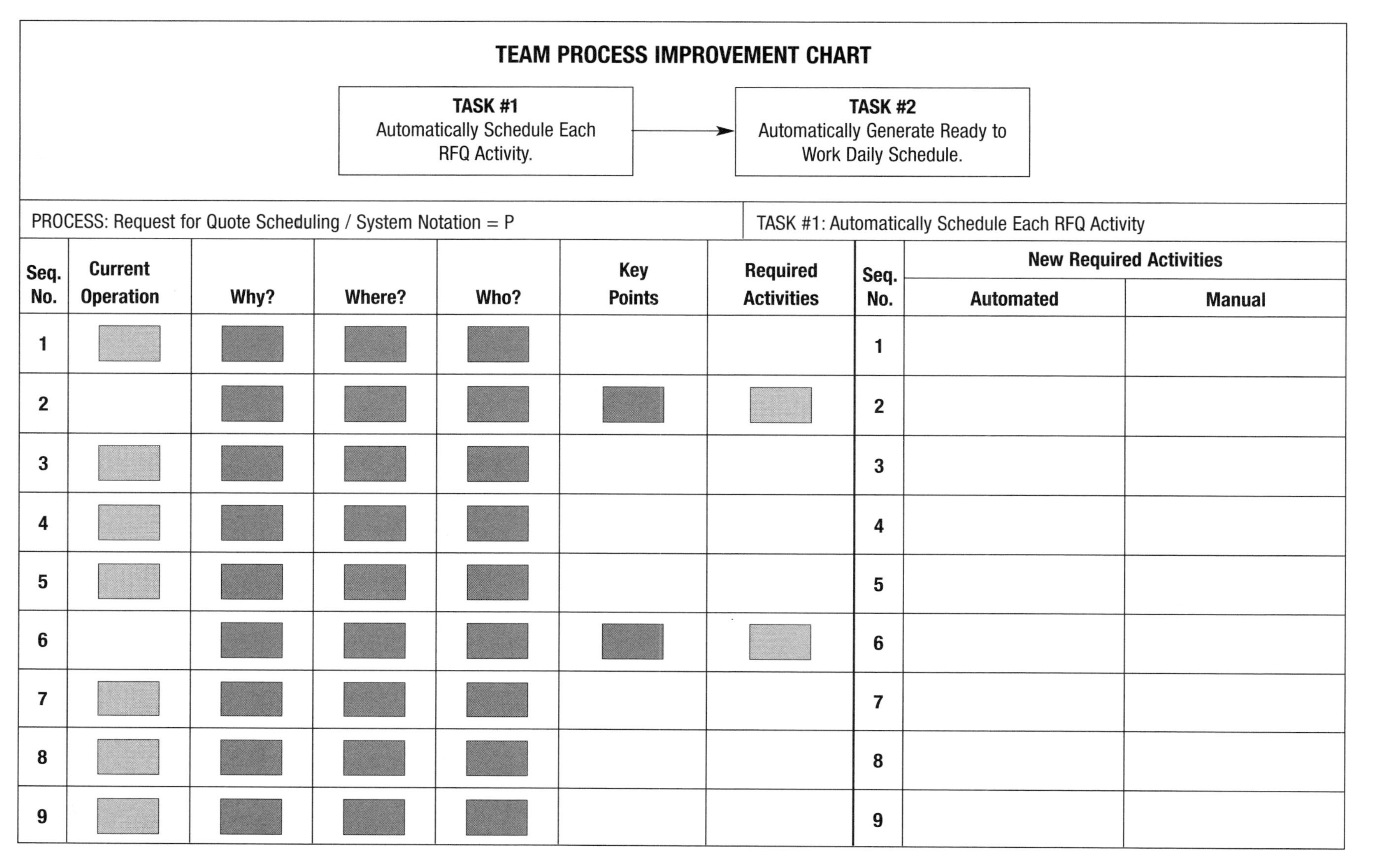

Figure 13-3. Team Process Improvement Chart

- **Required Activities:** The final step is to show which (if any) of the current operations will be retained. If a current operation needs to be retained, move the corresponding yellow sticky note from the current operation column to the required activities column. (See Figure 13-3.) These activities will be applied when creating "new required activities" on the right hand side of the chart.

If an entirely new process is to be created, the left-hand side of the chart is usually left blank. This, however, is not true when dealing with products that are related to aviation, nuclear, defense, and other industries subject to heavy government regulation. In such cases, it is advisable to fill out yellow sticky notes noting government regulations that pertain to the new task to ensure that nothing is overlooked in the development of this task.

The left-hand side of the chart makes everyone aware of the particulars of each operation that makes up the current task being reviewed for automation. The left-hand side makes waste highly visible, as defined and described in Chapter 2, and this waste must be eliminated before designing automation. (Only the required activities will remain when automated.)

Applying the Right-Hand Side of the Team Process Improvement Chart

The right-hand side of the chart is used to develop the new operations for the task (under "new required activities"). The BPI team brainstorms and reaches a consensus about each new operation, which is then noted on a 3″ × 3″ pink sticky note. This pink note will be placed in the appropriate sequence slot on the chart. (See Figure 13-4.) If the operation is to be automated, post the sticky-back note in the "automated" column; if the operation is to be manually performed, post it in the "manual" column.

It is important to remember that the objective is to automate each operation and that the vast majority of operations should fall into the automated category, with the exception of user input to initiate the program or user review required for specific adjustments for exceptions. Any other type of manual operation should be challenged because it can probably be automated. A task can be automated if the following is true:

- It is a repetitive process.
- A description of the step-by-step process can be verbalized.
- Data is made available.

Each task of the new process will have its own wall chart. Once the team defines the operations for each task, the individual task and associated operations will be transferred to the Future Process Sequence Chart. Once all the tasks for the process are completed, the BPI team is ready to select the system enhancement options.

The Magnum Example

At this time, the Magnum team had already agreed on the techniques that would be employed and had filled out the Technique Assessment Form. The next step was to

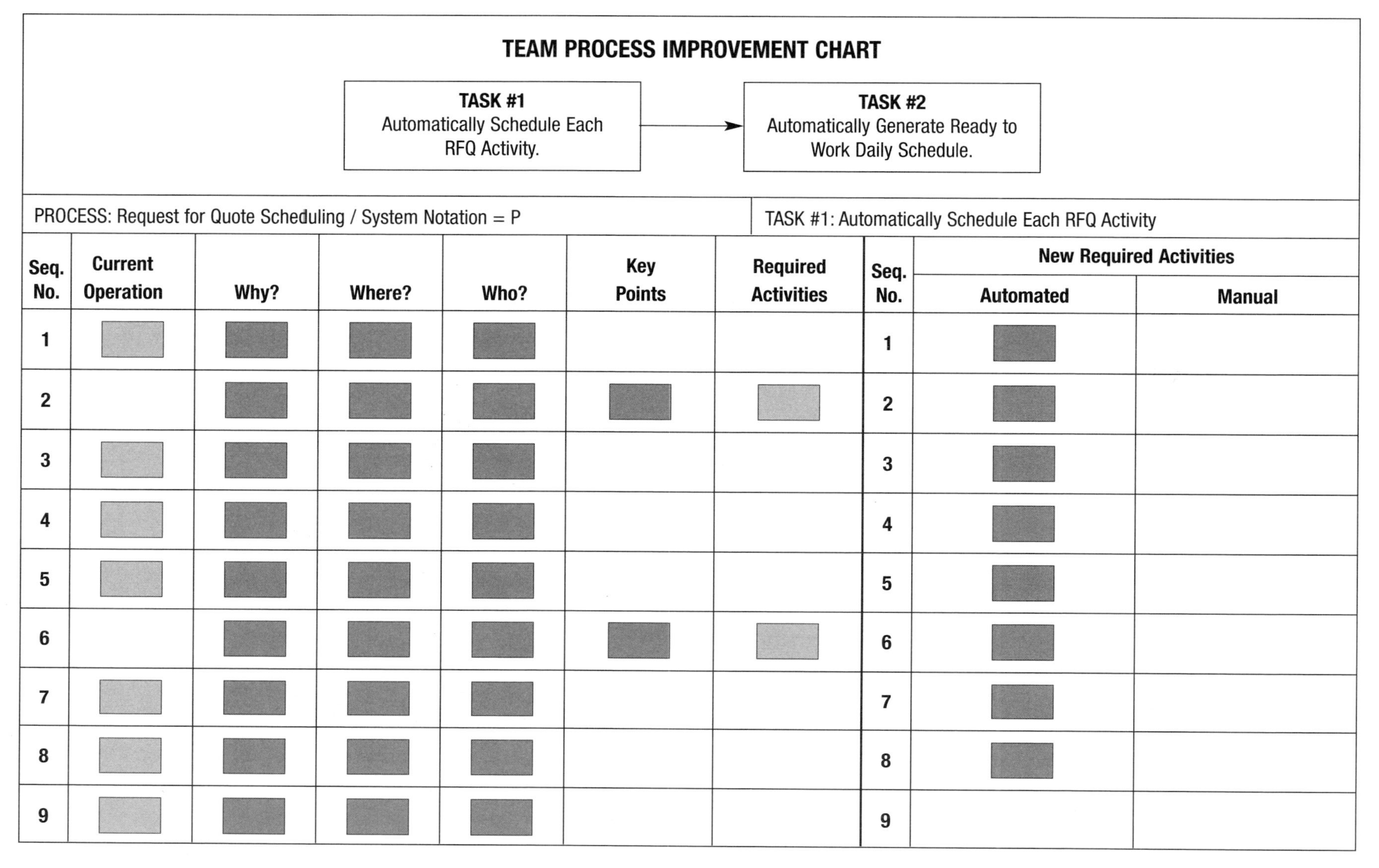

Figure 13-4. Team Process Improvement Chart – Right Side Application

complete a Team Process Improvement Chart and use the information from this chart to construct a Future Process Sequence Chart.

Filling Out the Top Part of the Team Process Improvement Chart

The Magnum BPI team entered the name of the process and the highest system notation from question 2: Partially Available (P).

The BPI team now focused on defining tasks. The materials expert led the discussion and recapped the three techniques everyone agreed should be implemented:

- Automatically calculate finish goods and component level order point
- Automatically trigger requirements based on consumption
- Automatically prioritize the triggered demand

She recommended that there be two tasks that embrace the above techniques.

- Task 1: Automatically calculate order point
- Task 2: Automatically trigger and prioritize the demand

The team agreed to the two tasks recommended by the materials expert and filled out the top portion of the Team Process Improvement Chart, as reflected in Figure 13-5.

Applying the Left-Hand Side of the Team Process Improvement Chart

The Magnum BPI team does not employ the left side of the Team Process Improvement Chart, since the current process of creating a master production schedule does not have anything to do with the new order point process.

Applying the Right-Hand Side of the Team Process Improvement Chart

The first task on this side of the chart was "automatically calculate order point." The materials expert explained to the BPI team the order point formula, which is (Average Daily Demand) (Lead Time + Safety Stock). Each of these elements is expressed in days or decimals of a day. She then explained the following:

- The automated system must first determine the average daily demand, then acquire the lead time, then the safety stock setting for each part number, and then apply the order point formula.
- The average daily demand for the environment should use historical demand, and then be adjusted up or down based upon the sales department forecasted sales dollars, which is fairly accurate.
- Customer booking history repeats itself with respect to product mix.

The team leader reminded team members that the task could be automated if

- it is a repetitive process;
- a description of the step-by-step process can be verbalized;
- data is made available.

TEAM PROCESS IMPROVEMENT CHART

TASK #1 Automatically Calculate Order Point. → **TASK #2** Automatically Trigger and Prioritize the Demand.

PROCESS: Order Point / System Nctation = P

TASK #1: Automatically Calculate Order Point

Seq. No.	Current Operation	Why?	Where?	Who?	Key Points	Required Activities	Seq. No.	New Required Activities	
								Automated	Manual
1							1		
2							2		
3							3		
4							4		
5							5		
6							6		
7							7		
8							8		
9							9		

Figure 13-5. Magnum's Team Process Improvement Chart: Top Portion Filled Out

The team started working on the first task (Task 1: Automatically calculate order point) and discussed the operations as if they were performing it manually. Their approach was as follows:

- Take the forecasted dollar amount to be shipped out this new month ($3,960,000) and divide it by the dollar amount shipped out the previous month ($3,600,000) to equal (1.10) a times factor. This times factor would be used for both the finish goods items and supporting components in the calculation of order points.
- Gather historical *sales quantities* for finish goods items and *historical usage quantities* for supporting component items going back one month in time.
- Divide each finish goods item part number's historical sales quantities and each supporting part number historical usage quantities by the number of manufacturing days (workdays) in the previous month to acquire an average daily demand for each part number.
- Then multiply the average daily demand by the times factor (1.10). This would increase or decrease the average daily demand in direct proportion to the anticipated current month sales increase or decrease.
- Take the anticipated average daily demand and multiply it by the total of lead time and safety stock, both expressed in day increments to equal the order point.

Once everyone was in agreement with the basic approach and that the calculations for this task were appropriate, the team was ready to define a step-by-step process starting with the first operation as if the user were employing the computer system. The team addressed each operation in the sequence it would be performed. Once each operation was agreed to, they wrote the operation on a pink sticky note and posted it on the Team Process Improvement Chart under the new required activities section. If the specific operation was to be a manual operation, the pink note went in the manual column; if the operation was to be automated, it went in the automated column. (See Figure 13-6.) This information was then entered on the Future Process Sequence Chart, shown in Figure 13-7. The team will save the Team Process Improvement Chart used for each task until the strategic objective has been achieved.

The team then obtained a new Team Process Improvement Chart and repeated the same process for task 2: Automatically trigger and prioritize the demand. After completing the Team Process Improvement Chart for this task, they again entered the information on the Future Process Sequence Chart. The next step was to fill in the estimated lead time to perform each of the individual tasks, the department that would be responsible for the task, staffing requirements, accumulated lead time to perform the process, and any key points. (See Figure 13-8.)

If the Technique Assessment Form was not filled out in answering question 2, the team gives a copy of the Future Process Sequence Chart to IT, which determines whether the current software package contains any of the required capabilities to automate the new

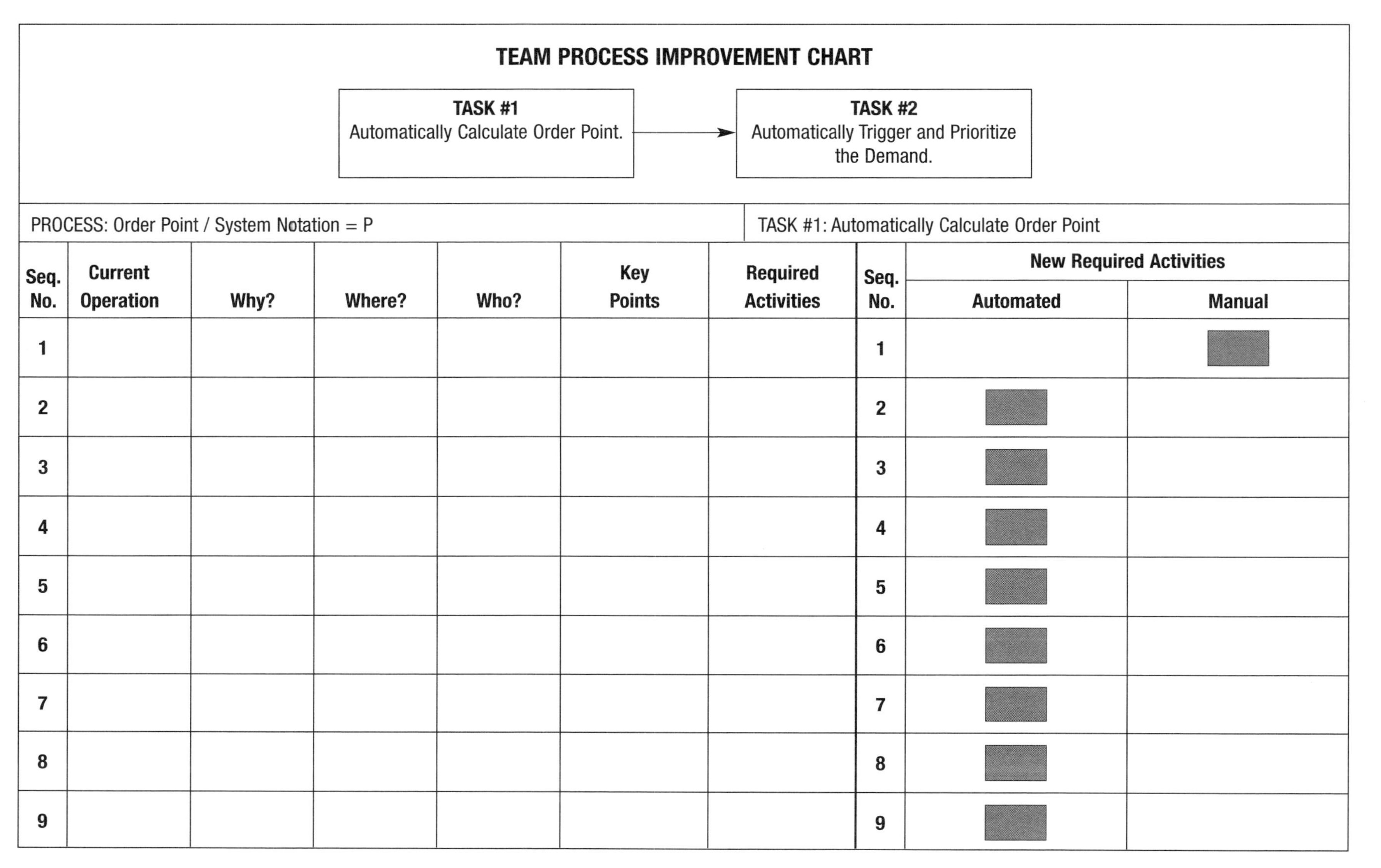

TEAM PROCESS IMPROVEMENT CHART

TASK #1
Automatically Calculate Order Point. → **TASK #2**
Automatically Trigger and Prioritize the Demand.

PROCESS: Order Point / System Notation = P | TASK #1: Automatically Calculate Order Point

Seq. No.	Current Operation	Why?	Where?	Who?	Key Points	Required Activities	Seq. No.	New Required Activities	
								Automated	Manual
1							1		
2							2		
3							3		
4							4		
5							5		
6							6		
7							7		
8							8		
9							9		

Figure 13-6. BPI Team Defines Operations for Automatically Calculating Order Points

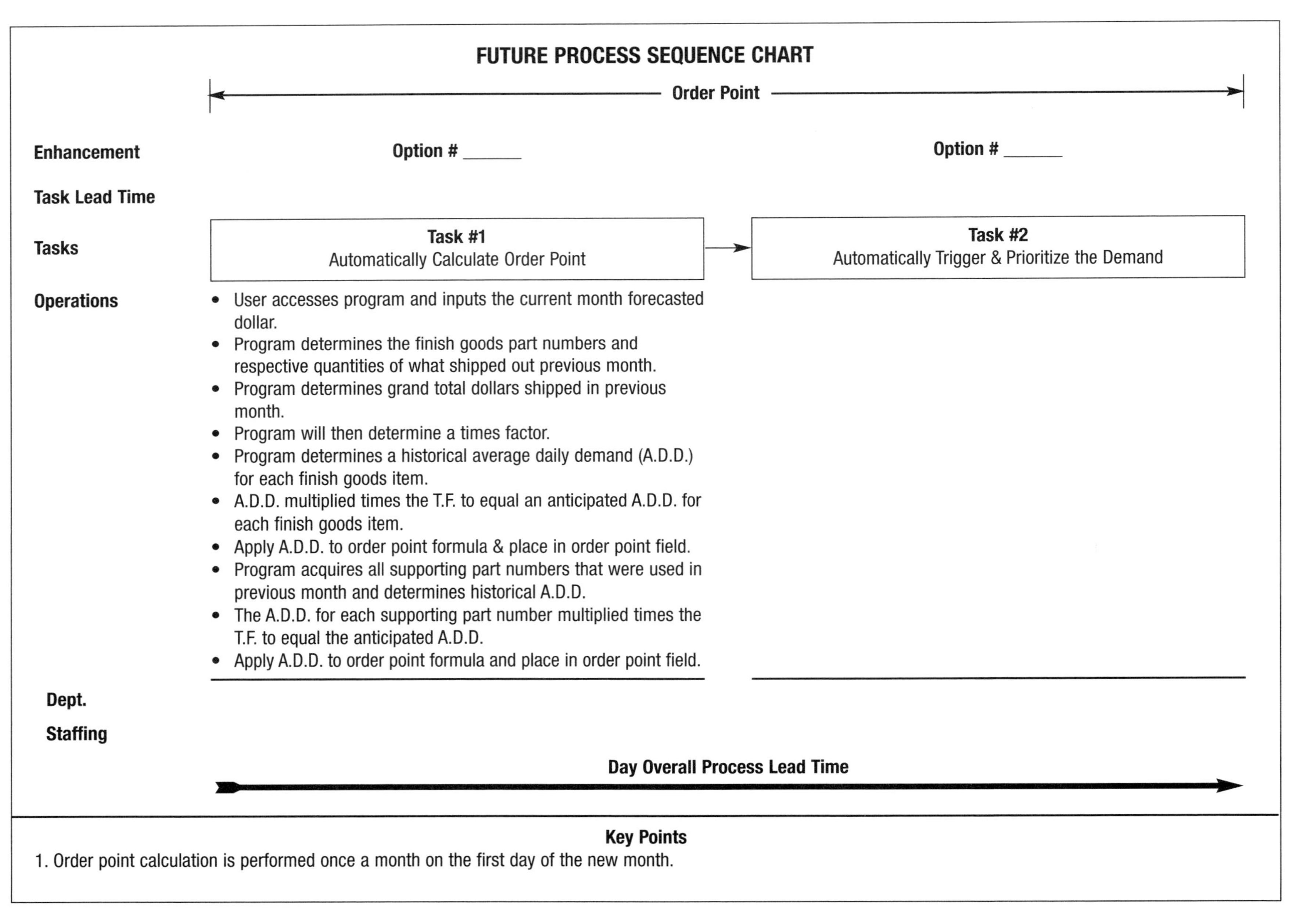

Figure 13-7. First Task Placed On Chart

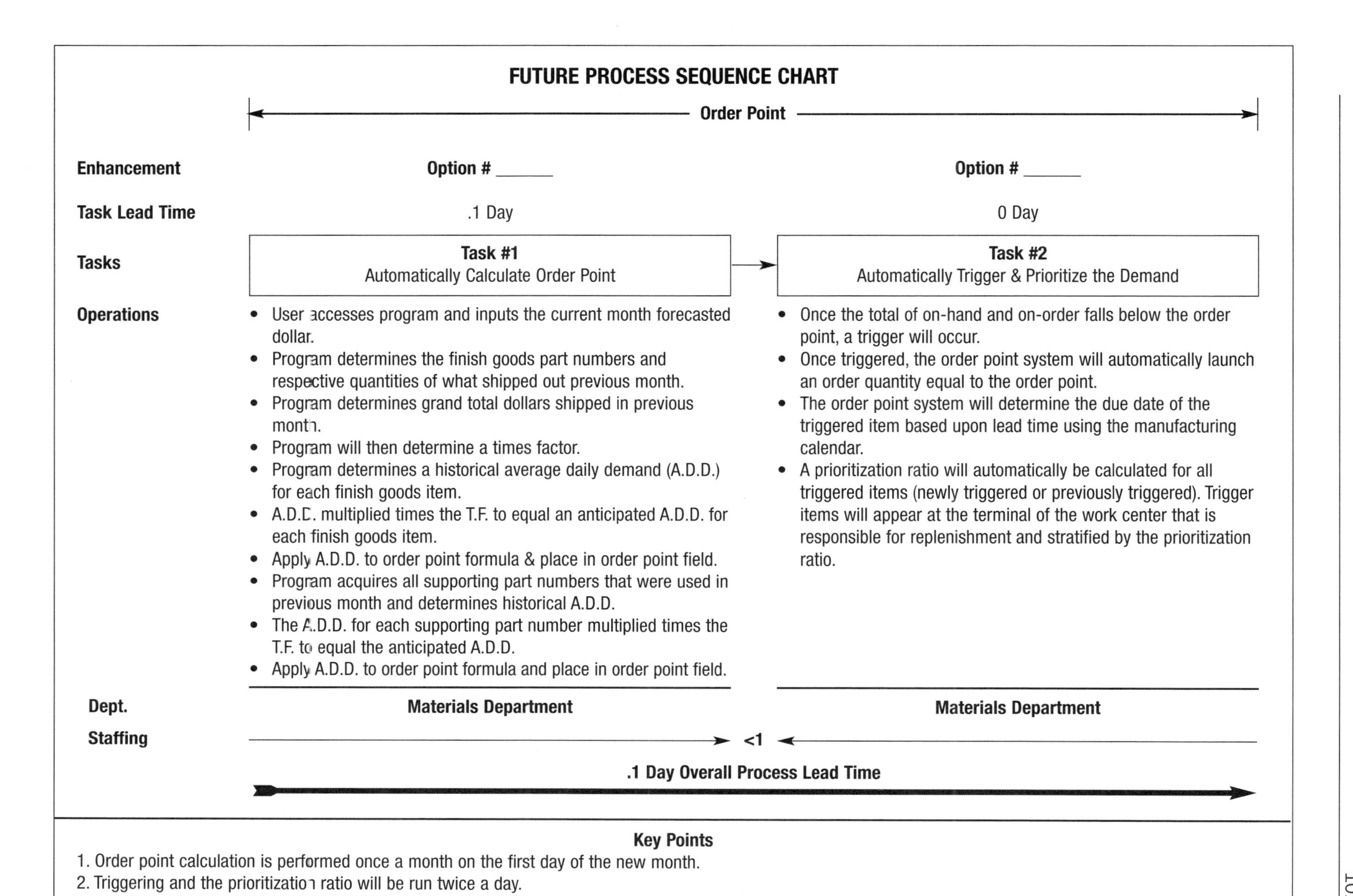

Figure 13-8. Second Task Placed On Chart

process. If this information is already available, the BPI team can move on to the next step in the sequence: selecting system enhancement options.

Selecting System Enhancement Option(s)

In this step, you will select the system enhancement option for each task displayed on the Future Process Sequence Chart. The system enhancement options that are available for adding, modifying or replacing system capabilities are discussed in Part Two, Chapters 4 through 8.

Often, more than one system enhancement can accomplish the automation. For example, if you want to automate the order entry process of incoming Web orders, you might choose to use system enhancement option two (bolt-on) or option four (custom routine). What you choose depends on conditions and issues discussed in the following sections.

Current System Capabilities

If the current system has all the capabilities desired and requires nothing more than configuration changes, this, of course, would be the first and easiest choice. The other relatively simple option is an extension hook, as the additional capability can typically be put into place relatively quickly and at a low cost, provided the resources are available to program the necessary routine.

Resources

If IT resources are not currently available (and cannot be made available) in your organization, you will have to rely on bolt-ons and on modification assistance from the supplier of the existing package. Custom routines, however, can often be outsourced.

Timing

If the project must be completed immediately, searching for and selecting a bolt-on would not work well in most cases because of the lead time required to make a proper selection. In this case, a custom routine may be quicker, provided the resources are immediately available. On the other hand, if time is not a major factor and programming resources are an issue, a bolt-on that meets your needs and is within your budget is the logical choice.

Cost

Cost, of course, is a major factor in the selection process. The tradeoffs between the system enhancement options from a cost standpoint have to be weighed.

Supplier's Willingness to Modify

If the supplier is willing to modify and continue to service the software per a service contract, and if the pricing is within budget, you might consider having the supplier make the required source code changes. If the supplier is unwilling to accommodate you, consider custom programming.

Each system enhancement option will have to be carefully reviewed and all of the factors listed above carefully weighed before a selection is made. The good news is that there is often more than one system enhancement option that can be applied to satisfy a specific need, and this gives you considerable flexibility.

At this point, we will return to the Magnum BPI team to illustrate how the system enhancement options are applied to the Future Process Sequence Chart, which has already been filled out with the agreed-upon tasks and operations, estimated lead time for each task, department responsibility for each task, estimated staffing, overall process lead time, and the key points of run frequency. The team will now select the system enhancement options that will be used to automate each task of the process. The BPI team leader suggested the following be taken into consideration in selecting the system enhancement options:

- When the system is turned on, we expect a larger than normal quantity of items triggered, as the system will increase finish goods levels to the proper levels. Currently, we have too much inventory for what we do not need and a large degree of shortfall on items we do need. The materials manager has performed a sample analysis, and based on the overall quantity that will be triggered in relationship to capacity, it will take one week to have the proper quantities on the shelf. We will try to build up the finish goods inventory from now until then; however, we should allow a week for proper adjustment of inventory.
- Today's date is January 23, 2009; our target date for achieving a 99 percent customer on-time delivery rate is March 27, 2009 (a Friday). On the evening of March 27, 2009, the measurement will be run to determine whether we have achieved a 99 percent customer on-time delivery rate for the week that begins on March 23, 2009 (a Monday). The required inventory has to be adjusted by the order point system the preceding week, Monday, March 16, 2009, through Friday, March 20, 2009. The system, therefore, needs to be in place and operating by March 13, 2009. This gives us seven weeks to have the order point system up and running.

The BPI team leader then went to the board and wrote down the five system enhancement options and asked for the team's input about selecting the system enhancement option:

- Option one: Software configuration settings
- Option two: Bolt-on
- Option three: Extension
- Option four: Supplier modifies source code
- Option five: Custom routines

The team discussed the system enhancement options and decided the following:

- The software configuration setting was not applicable to this situation.
- A bolt-on package would take too long (it would require the team to search, evaluate demos, acquire, write test procedures, perform test, write user operating procedures, train, and implement, and the time to accomplish all of these tasks was not available). Also, the likelihood of finding exactly what they needed would be slim due to the prioritization ratio required for their environment.
- The extension was not applicable since they currently did not have an order point module in place (only an order point field was available).
- The Supplier Modifies Source Code option was not applicable to this situation, as there was no order point module that required modification.
- The Custom Routine looked like the most promising option as it accommodated the tight timeline and the internal programming resources were available to program within a fairly short timeframe.

Thus, the team decided that the system enhancement option that it would employ for both tasks would be option five (custom routine). They wrote option five above the tasks on the Future Process Sequence Chart. (See Figure 13-9.)

Initiating Preliminary System Enhancement Option Action

System enhancement option(s), once selected, cannot begin to be implemented until executive approval is obtained. When it comes to expenditures and other resources, executive approval is typically required, and this is covered in Step 6. (See Chapter 15.) At this time, the system enhancement options selected need to be developed further to ensure it is a viable option from a technical, costs-benefit, and timing standpoint. The type of action required at this point in time is dependant upon the specific system enhancement option selected as reflected below:

Option One: Software Configuration Settings

This option requires further investigation by IT to ensure that it does not impact any other area of the system.

Option Two: Bolt-On

The team defines key requirements using the Future Process Sequence Chart as a guide. They fill out the Software Key Requirements Form, begin the supplier offerings research, obtain pricing and delivery lead-time information, schedule demos, perform reference checks, and select a package. (See Chapter 4.)

Option Three: Extension

The team defines step-by-step required enhancements, employing the Extension Worksheet. IT confirms that it can program the extension and estimates the lead-time required to program. (See Chapter 5.)

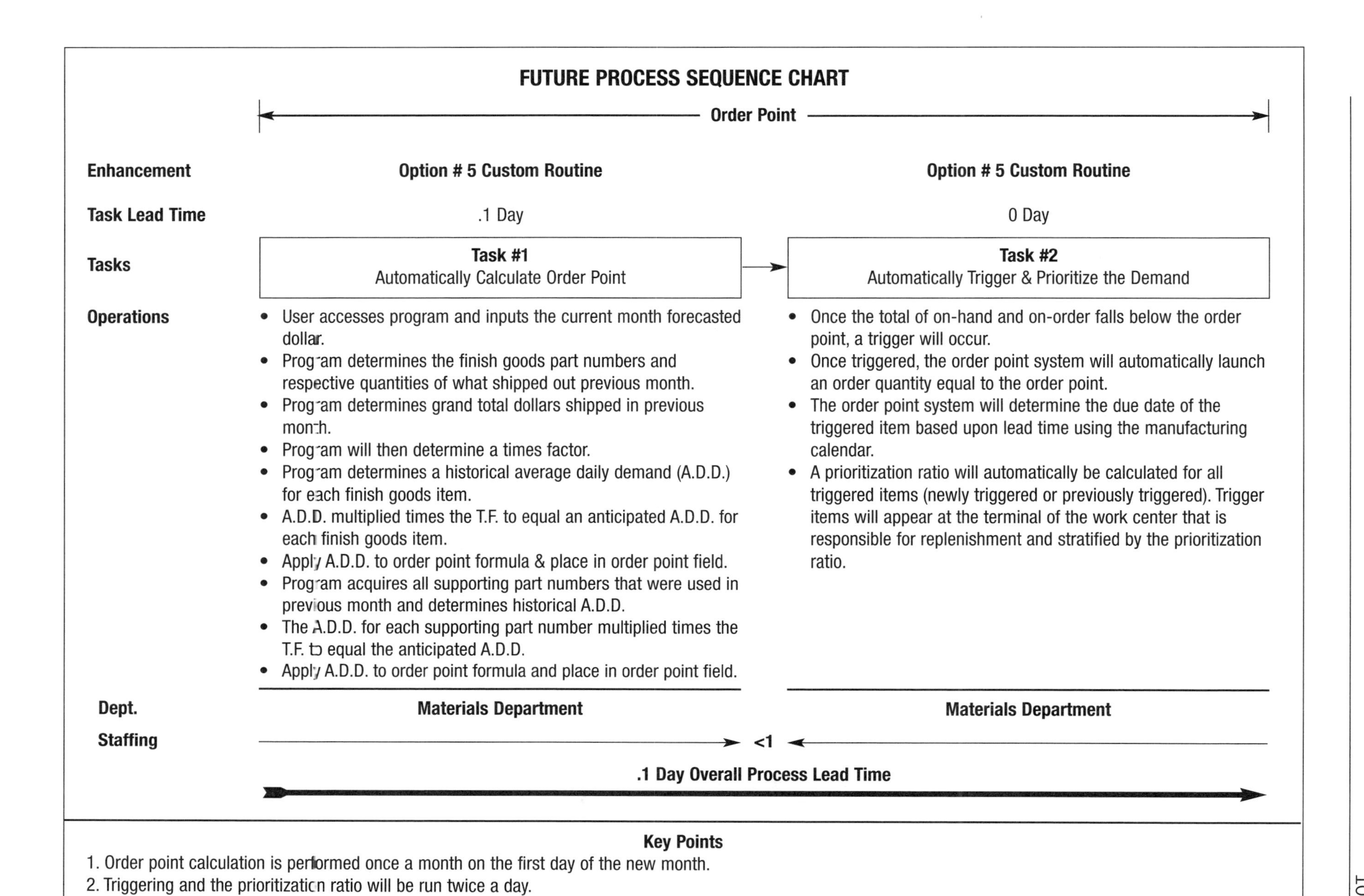

Figure 13-9. System Enhancement Option Selected

Option Four: Supplier Modifies Source Code

The team defines key requirements, determines the gaps, specs out the required modifications, and determines whether the supplier will make the customization, at what price and lead time, and whether the arrangement will include support after customization. (See Chapter 6.)

Option Five: Custom Routines

The team defines and demonstrates each step of the custom routine by applying the Custom Routine Design Worksheet. IT confirms that it can program the custom routine and estimates the lead time required to program. (See Chapter 7.)

It is important to understand that nothing is programmed, purchased, or switched on until executive approval is given, which follows a presentation of findings and recommendations. This step is only to ensure that the system enhancement options selected is viable from a technical, resource, costs-benefit and timing standpoint.

Magnum had already determined the tasks for its order point process, defined the operations for each task, and selected the system enhancement option of custom routine for both of its tasks. After the team entered all this information on its Future Process Sequence Chart, it was ready to create a document, which would be used to program the desired capabilities—the Custom Routine Design Worksheet (covered in Chapter 7). This worksheet provides the detail necessary to program the custom routine that is not available on the Future Process Sequence Chart, such as the design of the user input screen, output screen, and reports. In addition, it guides the user to gauge whether the data is currently available and, if not, to determine how it will become available. From an operation-by-operation standpoint, this worksheet adds the additional detail by demonstrating how each operation will function. In application, the Future Process Sequence Chart is the skeleton of the desired program and clearly shows the entire process. It is used as a good summary to communicate to all concerned what will occur and how it will occur, what departments will perform each task, expected overall process lead time to make it happen, and staffing requirements. It also serves as the basis for creating the Custom Routine Design Worksheet, Software Key Requirements Form, Extension Worksheet, and Supplier Modification Worksheet.

The Custom Routine Design Worksheets that the Magnum team created for the order point process (Task 1) is reflected in Figures 13-10a through 13-10e. The team then repeated the same process for the second task, "Automatically trigger and prioritize the triggered demand." (See Figures 13-11a through 13-11d.)

CUSTOM ROUTINE DESIGN WORKSHEET

Date	Team Leader	Team Members	
01/26/2009	Bob Smith	Janet Gains, Paul Johnson, Sam Peterson, Terry Hanson, and Adam Manner	Page 1 of 5

Task Name: Automatically Calculate Order Point	Process Name: Order Point

(Simply state, one operation at a time, the sequence in which the program will perform the operation, and demonstrate as required.)

1. The user will access the order point routine on the first work day of the new month and be prompted to input the current month "forecasted dollar." The user will then click on the "Calculate Order Point" button to engage the program. Example, today is February 2, 2009.

User Forecasted Dollar Input Example:
– $3,960,000 (For February)

2. The program will pick up each part number that is coded as a finish goods part number and then determine the total quantity shipped for each part number that occurred in the the previous month (e.g., January).

Finish Goods Part Number Total Quantity Shipped Previous Month Example

Finish Goods Part Number	Description	Total Qty Shipped
14C-234	Lock Pro	5,678
15B-167	Lock Right	4,390
16C-124	Lock Tight	6,122

3. The program will then pick up the current sales price and multiply it times the Total Quantity Shipped in January to equal the Extended Sales and then determine the Grand Total Dollars Shipped in January.

Grand Total Dollars Shipped Example

Finish Goods Part Number	Description	Current Sales Price	Total Qty Shipped	Extended Sales
14C-234	Lock Pro	5.75	5,678	$32,648.50
15B-167	Lock Right	7.25	4,390	$31,827.50
16C-124	Lock Tight	5.25	6,122	$32,140.50
Grand Total Dollars Shipped				$ 3,600,000

Figure 13-10a. Order Point Task Custom Routine Design Worksheets

CUSTOM ROUTINE DESIGN WORKSHEET

Date	Team Leader	Team Members	
01/26/2009	Bob Smith	Janet Gains, Paul Johnson, Sam Peterson, Terry Hanson, and Adam Manner	**Page 2 of 5**

Task Name: Automatically Calculate Order Point | Process Name: Order Point

4. Next, the program will determine a "Times Factor" by dividing the current months "Forecasted Dollar" by the "Grand Total Dollars Shipped"

Determine Times Factor Example

$3,960,000 Forecasted Dollar / $3,600,000 Grand Total Dollars Shipped = **1.1 Times Factor**

5. Next, the program will determine an "Historical Average Daily Demand" (A.D.D.) for each finish goods item that shipped in the previous month. It will take the "Total Quantity Shipped" for each finish goods item in the previous month and then divide it by the "Number of Manufacturing Days" (work days) there were in the previous month.

Previous Month Finish Goods Historical Average Daily Demand Example

Finish Goods Part Number	Description	Total Qty Shipped	Number of Manufacturing Days	Historical Average Daily Demand
14C-234	Lock Pro	5,678	22	258.1
15B-167	Lock Right	4,390	22	199.5
16C-124	Lock Tight	6,122	22	278.3

6. Next, the program will multiply the "Historical Average Daily Demand" times the "Times Factor" to equal a "Anticipated Average Daily Demand." Round to nearest whole number.

Current Month Finish Goods Anticipated Average Daily Demand Example

Finish Goods Part Number	Description	Historical Average Daily Demand	Times Factor	Anticipated Average Daily Demand
14C-234	Lock Pro	258.1	1.1	284
15B-167	Lock Right	199.5	1.1	219
16C-124	Lock Tight	278.3	1.1	306

Figure 13-10b. Order Point Task Custom Routine Design Worksheets

CUSTOM ROUTINE DESIGN WORKSHEET

Date	Team Leader	Team Members	
01/26/2009	Bob Smith	Janet Gains, Paul Johnson, Sam Peterson, Terry Hanson, and Adam Manner	Page 3 of 5

Task Name: Automatically Calculate Order Point	Process Name: Order Point

7. Next, the "Anticipated A.D.D." is then applied to the order point formula to determine the finish goods order point for the current month. The formula is: (Average Daily Demand) (Lead Time + Safety Stock). The lead time and safety stock is expressed in days or decimal of a day. The order point is rounded to the nearest whole number. The user will be given a screen to review the order points and be given override capability. Once the user has completed the review they will click on the "Load Order Point" button, which will populate the order point fields with the new order points.

Finish Goods Order Point Calculation Example

Supporting Part Number	Description	Anticipate Average Daily Demand	Lead Time	Safety Stock	Current Month Order Point
14C-234	Lock Pro	284	2	1	852
15B-167	Lock Right	219	2	1	657
16C-124	Lock Tight	306	2	1	918

8. Next, the program will determine a "Historical Month Average Daily Demand" for each supporting item that was used in the previous month. It will take the "Total Quantity Used" for each supporting item in the previous month (e.g., January) and then divide it by the "Number of Manufacturing Days" (work days) there were in the previous month. Round to nearest tenth.

Supporting Part Number	Description	Total Qty Used	Number of Manufacturing Days	Historical Average Daily Demand
23245	Strike Plate	39,000	22	1,772.7
32434	Strike Plate	12,345	22	561.1
36782	Strike Plate	9,345	22	424.8

Figure 13-10c. Order Point Task Custom Routine Design Worksheets

CUSTOM ROUTINE DESIGN WORKSHEET

Date	Team Leader	Team Members	
01/26/2009	Bob Smith	Janet Gains, Paul Johnson, Sam Peterson, Terry Hanson, and Adam Manner	Page 4 of 5

Task Name: Automatically Calculate Order Point | Process Name: Order Point

9. Next, multiply the “Historical Month Average Daily Demand” by the “Times Factor” that calculated for the finish goods level to equal a “Anticipated Average Daily Demand.” Round to nearest whole number.

Supporting Part Number	Description	Historical Average Daily Demand	Times Factor	Anticipated Average Daily Demand
23245	Strike Plate	1,772.7	1.1	1,950
32434	Strike Plate	561.1	1.1	617
36782	Strike Plate	424.8	1.1	467

10. Next, the program will take the “Anticipated Average Daily Demand” for each supporting component and then apply it to the order point formula to determine the “Current Month Order Point” for the components for the current month. The formula is: (Average daily demand) (Lead Time + Safety Stock). The “Lead Time” and “Safety Stock” are expressed in days or decimal of a day. The user will be given a screen to review the order points and be given override capability. Once the user has completed the review, they will click on the “Load Order Point” button, which will populate the order point fields with the new order points.

Component Level Order Point Calculation Example

Supporting Part Number	Description	Anticipated Average Daily Demand	Lead Time	Safety Stock	Current Month Order Point
23245	Strike Plate	1,950	2	1	5,850
32434	Strike Plate	617	2	1	1,851
36782	Strike Plate	467	2	1	1,401

Figure 13-10d. Order Point Task Custom Routine Design Worksheets

CUSTOM ROUTINE DESIGN WORKSHEET

Date	Team Leader	Team Members	
01/26/2009	Bob Smith	Janet Gains, Paul Johnson, Sam Peterson, Terry Hanson, and Adam Manner	Page 5 of 5

Task Name: Automatically Calculate Order Point | Process Name: Order Point

(Design the users' input screen, output screen, and reports, as required)

Input Screen

$3,960,000 **Current Month Forecasted Dollar**

Calculate Order Point

Output Screen & Report

Load Order Point

Supporting Part Number	Description	Current Month Average Daily Demand	Lead Time	Safety Stock	Current Month Order Point
23245	Strike Plate	1,950	2	1	5,850
32434	Strike Plate	617	2	1	1,851
36782	Strike Plate	467	2	1	1,401

1. There will be one screen for finish goods and one screen for supporting components placed in part number sequence. From the screen, the user can change a calculated order point.
2. There will be search capability by part number.

(Determine the program's data requirements, if available, and if accurate.)

Data Required:

Part Number: OK Description OK Historical Finish Goods Shipments by Day: OK Inventory Classification Code: OK Historical Component Usage By Day: OK
Lead Time: OK Safety Stock: OK

——— END ORDER POINT TASK ———

Figure 13-10e. Order Point Task Custom Routine Design Worksheets

CUSTOM ROUTINE DESIGN WORKSHEET

Date	Team Leader	Team Members	
01/26/2009	Bob Smith	Janet Gains, Paul Johnson, Sam Peterson, Terry Hanson, and Adam Manner	Page 1 of 4

Task Name: Automatically Trigger & Prioritize the Demand | Process Name: Order Point

(Simply state, one operation at a time, the sequence in which the program will perform the operation, and demonstrate as required.)

1. The system will continuously monitor the total of "On-Hand" inventory and "On-Order" as it compares with the "Order Point." If the total of "On-Hand" inventory plus "On-Order" fall below the "Order Point" a "Trigger" will occur.

Example:

Part Number	Description	Item Type	Order Point	On Hand	On Order	Total	Trigger
14C-234	Lock Pro	Finish Goods	852	840	0	840	Yes
15B-167	Lock Right	Finish Goods	657	325	600	925	No
16C-124	Lock Tight	Finish Goods	918	600	0	600	Yes
23245	Strike Plate	Component	5,850	4,000	2,000	6,000	No
32434	Strike Plate	Component	1,851	1,200	0	1,200	Yes
36782	Strike Plate	Component	1,401	1,300	1,000	2,300	No

2. Once triggered, the system will launch the full "Order Quantity" (Order quantity equals order point).

Example:

Part Number	Description	Item Type	Order Point	On Hand	On Order	Total	Trigger	Launch Order Qty
14C-234	Lock Pro	Finish Goods	852	840	0	840	Yes	852
15B-167	Lock Right	Finish Goods	657	325	600	925	No	–
16C-124	Lock Tight	Finish Goods	918	600	0	600	Yes	918
23245	Strike Plate	Component	5,850	4,000	2,000	6,000	No	–
32434	Strike Plate	Component	1,851	1,200	0	1,200	Yes	1,851
36782	Strike Plate	Component	1,401	1,300	1,000	2,300	No	–

Figure 13-11a. Automatically Trigger and Prioritize the Demand Task: Custom Routine Design Worksheets

CUSTOM ROUTINE DESIGN WORKSHEET

Date	**Team Leader**	**Team Members**	
01/26/2009	Bob Smith	Janet Gains, Paul Johnson, Sam Peterson, Terry Hanson, and Adam Manner	**Page 2 of 4**

Task Name: Automatically Trigger & Prioritize the Demand | Process Name: Order Point

(Simply state, one operation at a time, in the sequence in which the program will perform the operation, and demonstrate as required.)

3) The order point system will determine the "Due Date" of the triggered item based upon "Lead Time" using the manufacturing calendar.

Example: Today is 2/2/2009, all lead times are 2 days and these items just triggered.

Part Number	Description	Item Type	Order Point	On Hand	On Order	Total	Trigger	Launch Order Qty	Due Date
14C-234	Lock Pro	Finish Goods	852	840	0	840	Yes	852	2/4/2009
16C-124	Lock Tight	Finish Goods	918	600	0	600	Yes	918	2/4/2009
32434	Strike Plate	Component	1,851	1,200	0	1,200	Yes	1,851	2/4/2009

4. A "Prioritization Ratio" will automatically be calculated for each item that has been triggered and well as those items that have previously triggered (current open work orders). It is determined by dividing the "On-Hand" quantity by the "Order Point." Retain only two decimal places.

Example: Determine prioritization ratio for newly triggered items and previously triggered items that still have an open work order.

Part Number	Description	Item Type	Order Point	On Hand	On Order	Total	Trigger	Launch Order Qty	Due Date	Prioritization Ratio	
14C-234	Lock Pro	Finish Goods	852	840	0	840	Yes	852	2/4/2009	.98	Just Triggered
16C-124	Lock Tight	Finish Goods	918	600	0	600	Yes	918	2/4/2009	.65	
32434	Strike Plate	Component	1,851	1,200	0	1,200	Yes	1,851	2/4/2009	.64	
15B-167	Lock Right	Finish Goods	657	325	600	925	No		2/3/2009	.49	Previously Triggered
23245	Strike Plate	Component	5,850	4,000	2,000	6,000	No		2/3/2009	.68	
36782	Strike Plate	Component	1,401	1,300	1,000	2,300	No		2/3/2009	.92	

5. The Trigger items will appear at the terminal of the work center that is responsible for replenishment and stratified by the prioritization ratio. See output screen on next page for example.

Figure 13-11b. Automatically Trigger and Prioritize the Demand Task: Custom Routine Design Worksheets

CUSTOM ROUTINE DESIGN WORKSHEET

Date	Team Leader	Team Members	
01/26/2009	Bob Smith	Janet Gains, Paul Johnson, Sam Peterson, Terry Hanson, and Adam Manner	Page 3 of 4

Task Name: Automatically Trigger & Prioritize the Demand | Process Name: Order Point

(Design the users' input screen, output screen, and reports, as required)

Input Screen

■ **Nothing required.**

Output Screen & Report

WORK CENTER 22: FINISH GOODS

Part Number	Description	Order Quantity	Due Date	Ratio
15B-167	Lock Right	600	2/3/2009	.49
16C-124	Lock Tight	918	2/4/2009	.65
14C-234	Lock Pro	840	2/4/2009	.98

WORK CENTER 28: COMPONENT STAMPING

Part Number	Description	Order Quantity	Due Date	Ratio
32434	Strike Plate	1,851	2/4/2009	.64
23245	Strike Plate	6,000	2/3/2009	.68
36782	Strike Plate	2,300	2/3/2009	.92

- All items will be segmented by work center and appear on the terminal at each work center. **The trigger demand will be stratified by the prioritization ratio regardless of due date**.
- **The prioritization ratio will be run twice a day automatically: 7:00 AM and 12:00 PM**
- There will be report capability segmented in the same fashion as the screen capability.

Figure 13-11c. Automatically Trigger and Prioritize the Demand Task: Custom Routine Design Worksheets

CUSTOM ROUTINE DESIGN WORKSHEET			
Date 01/26/2009	**Team Leader** Bob Smith	**Team Members** Janet Gains, Paul Johnson, Sam Peterson, Terry Hanson, and Adam Manner	**Page 4 of 4**
Task Name: Automatically Trigger & Prioritize the Demand		Process Name: Order Point	

(Determine the program's data requirements, if it is available, and if it is accurate.)

Data Required:

Part Number: OK **Description: OK** **On-Hand Inventory: OK** **On-Order: OK**
Lead Time: OK **Work Center: OK** **Order Point: OK**

——— END AUTOMATICALLY TRIGGER & PRIORITIZE THE DEMAND TASK ———

Figure 13-11d. Automatically Trigger and Prioritize the Demand Task: Custom Routine Design Worksheets

Additional Key Point

Prior to applying Step 4, it is vital to understand the definition of office waste and the thirteen forms of wastes that are typically found in the office (see Chapter 2). This ensures that waste is identified and eliminated in the determination of required activities.

Step 5: Preparing for Implementation

14

In this step, the BPI team will construct an Implementation Milestone Chart and a cost-benefit analysis.

Constructing an Implementation Milestone Chart

Every BPI team member should participate in the process of constructing the Implementation Milestone Chart. This way, everyone will not only understand what must be done but also why it must be done. The Implementation Milestone Chart is critical to successful implementation for the following reasons:

- It provides a well-thought-out plan, step-by-step, of what must be accomplished. Without this plan, important steps will be overlooked. These oversights can impact the timeline and/or the success of the overall project.
- The commitment date for task completion comes from the team member who is assigned the responsibility of completing the milestone task. This individual is the only person who can commit to a date because he or she is the only one who knows their overall workload (if not 100 percent dedicated to the administration automation project) and the degree of effort required to perform the assigned task. If the anticipated completion date given for the task will have an impact on the required completion date of the project, it is best to know it up front so that alternatives can be considered.
- The process of laying out the Implementation Milestone Chart brings the BPI team to a whole new level of understanding. It provides the insight necessary for success.
- The Implementation Milestone Chart serves as a constant reminder of what must be done, by when, by whom. Nothing is left to memory; the chart is constantly reviewed during regularly scheduled team meetings, attended by all, to ensure that the project is going according to plan.

The BPI team must also remember that system enhancements are supported by such activities as developing procedures, training, acquiring equipment, testing, measuring, and reporting. Equally important are the balance of other administration automation steps, which include:

- Cost-benefit analysis
- Executive presentation/approval to implement
- Secondary measurements

Figure 14-1 illustrates the basic Implementation Milestone Chart format. The information required for each numbered section of the figure is listed below:

1. The team member's initials to cross-reference with their name. Initials are entered in the "assign to" column of the form (also see #6), reflecting who is responsible for the task. There can be multiple team members involved with a specific task and there may not be room to spell out everyone's name in the "assigned to" column. The cross-reference of initials to name is available to ensure there is no confusion as to who is responsible for the task.
2. Date and page numbers.
3. The objective. This is the objective that the tasks listed below are to accomplish.
4. All tasks are numbered for easy identification, and the number assigned for each task is entered here.
5. The specific task name.
6. The initial of the individual(s) responsible for the task (also see #1).
7. The expected completion date for the task.
8. The actual completion date.
9. The week ending (Friday) dates.
10. Symbols showing that a task has been planned, started, or completed. These are the symbols used to denote:
    - Planned start of the task (circle not filled in)
    - Actual start of the task (circle filled in)
    - Planned completion of the task (triangle not filled in)
    - Actual completion of the task (triangle filled in).

System Enhancement Implementation Steps and the Implementation Milestone Chart

All steps required for implementation of selected system enhancement options should be included in the Implementation Milestone Chart. This includes any tasks related to achieving the desired capabilities for each system enhancement option selected.

- **Test the program.** Whether you have selected bolt-on, supplier modification, extension, or a custom routine, it must be tested. Moreover, you should know what the outcome of the test will be before testing. In other words, the data is preset, and each function is performed to see whether the program yields the intended results. If the

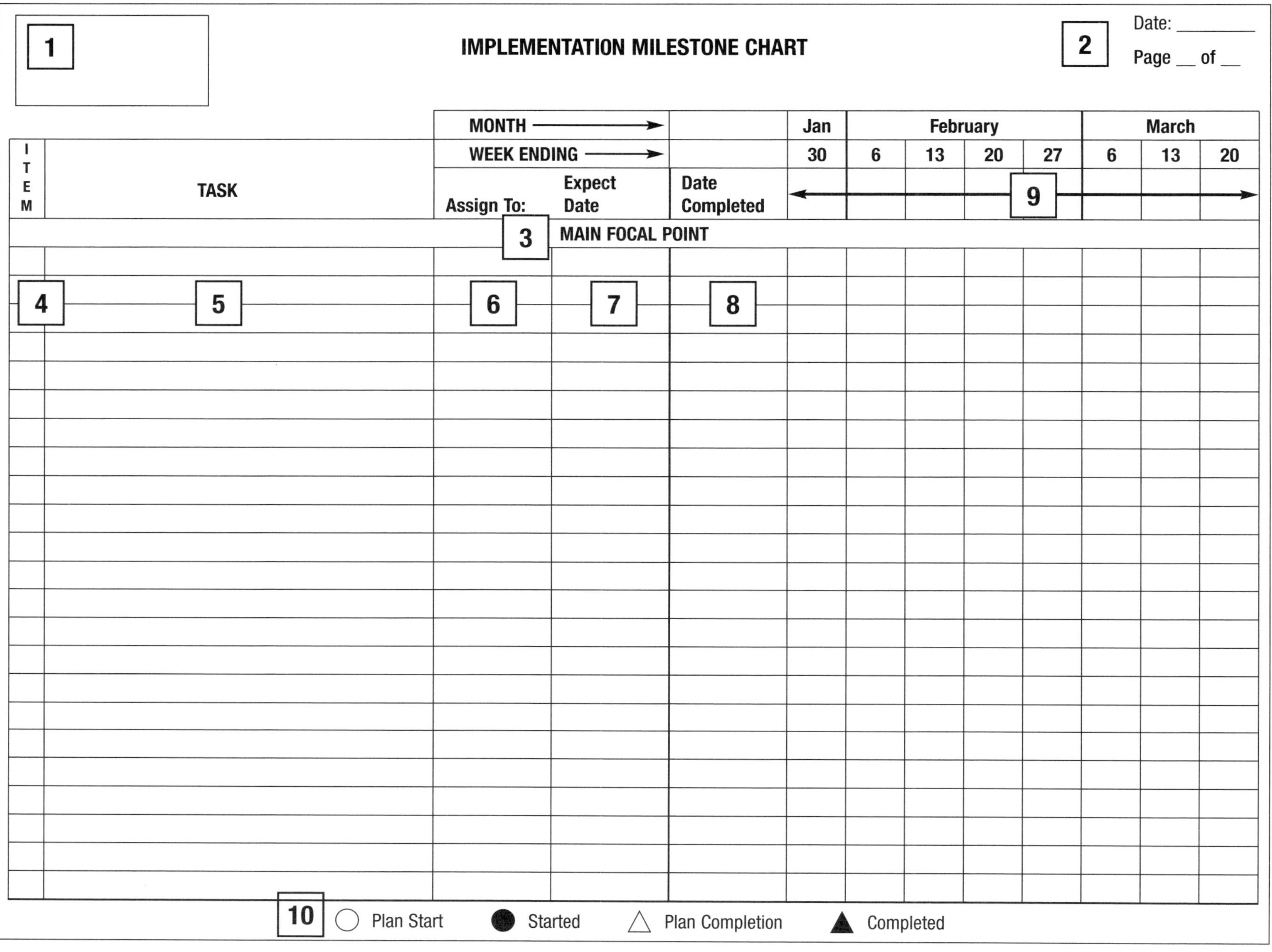

Figure 14-1. Implementation Milestone Chart

test is not performed in this manner, there is little hope of catching bugs (which almost certainly exist), regardless of where the program came from.

- **Write user operating procedures.** The main reason manual or automated systems go bad is *exceptions*. All procedures, therefore, should describe how to apply the system as well as how to handle the exceptions.
- **Train all users.** The training should first cover the overall process that is being put into place and then how each user will interface and apply their portion of the system. By understanding the whole process the user is in a better position to make informed decisions on their portion of the system on a day-to-day basis.
- **Procure and install equipment.** There are often numerous steps involved in procuring and installing equipment. This may involve purchasing equipment from multiple sources, coordinating with subcontractors, and testing both the equipment and installation. With all the activity and disruptions that occur on a day-to-day basis, it is best to include all the required steps on the Implementation Milestone Chart to ensure nothing is overlooked.

Figure 14-2 shows the Implementation Milestone Chart filled in by the Magnum BPI team. The chart includes all of the components described above and clearly shows the main tasks, the status of each task, planned and actual start and completion dates, and the people involved in the process.

Once the Implementation Milestone Chart is completed, the team then doublechecks it to ensure that

- all the required tasks have been listed, and that nothing needs to be modified or eliminated;
- everyone feels comfortable with the assigned task(s) and agrees to the timelines.

Cost-Benefit Analysis

Waste and non-value-added activities abound in most office environments and, typically, a good portion of this waste has to do with the mismatch between the processes in place (dictated by the current off-the-shelf computer system) and what the organization needs to have in place to compete successfully. Implementing any other set of techniques other than administration automation to the office greatly minimizes the full benefits that could be realized, even if they were able to eliminate the most obvious aspects of waste. The reason is simply that the required activities are still being performed manually. With administration automation the processes are tailored to meet the specific needs of the environment and the required activities are then automated.

Although the team is aware that significant competitive gains can be achieved, it would be pointless to attempt to acquire approval to implement unless a cost-benefit analysis is presented. Not only must the cost-benefit analysis be presented, but it should be reviewed by the company controller prior to being presented to management. The controller

B = Bob S = Sam
J = Janet T = Terry
P = Paul A = Adam

IMPLEMENTATION MILESTONE CHART

Date: 1/30/2009

Page 1 of 1

ITEM	TASK	Assign To:	Expect Date	Date Completed	Jan 30	February 6	February 13	February 20	February 27	March 6	March 13	March 20
	ADMINISTRATION AUTOMATION ACTIVITIES											
1	Perform cost-benefit analysis	Team	2/04/2009			○△						
2	Executive presentation/approval to implement	Team	2/06/2009			○△						
3	Determine secondary measurements	Team	2/13/2009				○△					
4	Put secondary measurements in place	A	2/20/2009					○△				
	COMPUTER TERMINALS INSTALLED AT EACH WORK CENTER											
1	Procure terminals	P	2/09/2009				○△					
2	Have contractors install cable	P	2/13/2009				○△					
3	Receive & install terminals	P	2/18/2009					○△				
4	Test equipment and installation	P	2/19/2009									
	AUTOMATICALLY CALCULATE ORDER POINT / TRIGGER & PRIORITIZE THE DEMAND											
1	Complete custom routine design worksheet	Team	1/29/2009	1/29/2009	●▲							
2	Program in-house	P	2/20/2009				○	△				
3	Write program test procedures	J/S	2/20/2009				○	△				
4	Test & debug	J/S/P	3/06/2009						○	△		
5	Write user operating procedures	T/A	2/20/2009				○	△				
6	Train	Team	3/09/2009								○△	
7	Implement	Team	3/10/2009								△	

○ Plan Start ● Started △ Plan Completion ▲ Completed

Figure 14-2. Magnum's Implementation Milestone Chart

checks the analysis to ensure that all appropriate costs and benefits have been accurately identified and calculated.

Once the analysis passes the controller's scrutiny, the information should be organized in an easy-to-understand format that management can review. The form used to summarize and present the costs-benefits is shown in Figure 14-3. The following information must be included:

A. Team leader's name
B. Team members
C. Current date
D. Page number
E. Strategic objective or executive mandate given
F. The root cause issue(s)
G. Recommended solution(s)
H. Major changes that will take place
I. The individual items and their cost (also total cost)
J. All the anticipated benefits and their savings (and a total dollar benefit)
K. Expected net savings (subtract the total costs from the total dollar benefits)
L. Date when the strategic objective will be achieved
M. Any necessary comments

Magnum's BPI team knew that the cost-benefit analysis would be the focal point of its presentation to management and that getting the approval and the funds for implementation relied on persuasive, well-organized data. By this point, the BPI team had designed both custom routines and developed its Implementation Milestone Chart and was ready to estimate the costs and benefits of implementing the order point system. The BPI team had agreed that each work center should have a computer terminal from which updates can be obtained several times a day. The IT supervisor and the materials manager each had conducted an analysis and their findings are presented below.

IT Supervisor's Perspective

There are ten work centers, so we need ten computer terminals. We need to have cable laid in, plus we need hardware. It will cost $4,000 for the terminals, $1,000 for hardware, and $5,000 to have the cable installed by an outside contractor. Total cost equals $10,000.

Materials Manager's Perspective

I sampled 350 high- and low-volume part numbers and believe that the following is true:

- Our current finish goods inventory is at $2,000,000. It will increase initially by 20 percent ($400,000), and then, overall, will drop 22 percent ($440,000) below today's

COST-BENEFIT ANALYSIS

Team Leader: ______ A ______

Team Members: ______ B ______

C Date: ______

D Page ___ of ___

E. Strategic Objective :

F. Root Cause Issue(s):

G. Recommended Solution(s):

H. Major Changes Expected:

I. Total Cost:

J. Total Benefits:

K. Net Savings:

L. Date to Achieve Strategic Objective:

M. Comments:

Figure 14-3. Cost-Benefit Analysis Form

current levels within sixteen weeks. The end result would equate to a $440,000 drop in finish goods inventory. At a 25 percent carrying cost, this would equal a reduction in cost of $110,000.

- Our current component level inventory is at $5,000,000. It will increase initially by 8 percent ($400,000), and then overall would drop by 26 percent ($1,300,000) below today's current levels within sixteen weeks. The end result would equate to a $1,300,000 drop in component inventory. At a 25 percent carrying cost, this would equal a reduction of cost of $325,000. Work in process will increase by 8 percent but would then go back to current levels within a week. This would equate to a zero difference in work-in-process inventory levels.
- The component level shortage rate is currently at 1 percent, and I believe it will stay at the same level.

Total reduction in inventory would equal a savings of $435,000.

Next Steps

The team then filled out the cost-benefit form as reflected in Figures 14-4a through 14-4c and reviewed it with the executive sponsor and the controller to ensure accuracy.

Additional Key Point

The Implementation Milestone Chart is a living document to which tasks can be added as required, and it is reviewed and updated by the team on an ongoing basis until the implementation is completed.

COST-BENEFIT ANALYSIS

Team Leader: Bob Smith

Team Members: Janet Gains, Paul Johnson, Sam Peterson, Terry Hanson, and Adam Manner

Date: February 4, 2009

Page **1 of 3**

Strategic Objective #1:

We will increase our customer on-time delivery from 75% to 99%+ by March 27, 2009.

Root Cause Issue(s):

- We lack automated tools for generating a master production schedule.

Recommended Solution(s):

- Automatically calculate finish goods and component level order point.
- Automatically trigger requirements based upon consumption.
- Automatically prioritize the triggered demand.

Major Changes Expected:

- Going from a push methodology to a pull methodology. Pull methodology is highly responsive to actual customer orders and component consumption.
- Prioritization methodology ensures the right items are being worked on during the course of each day.
- Each work center will have a computer terminal to guide production throughout the facility. This permits several updates per day as to what should be worked on as customer orders are shipped and consumption occurs throughout the day.

Figure 14-4a. Magnum's Cost-Benefit Analysis

COST-BENEFIT ANALYSIS

Team Leader: Bob Smith

Date: February 4, 2009

Team Members: Janet Gains, Paul Johnson, Sam Peterson, Terry Hanson, and Adam Manner

Page **2 of 3**

Total Costs:

$4,000 Ten terminals
$1,000 Hardware
$5,000 Install cable
$10,000 Total Costs

Total Benefits:

$110,000 Finish goods inventory carrying cost savings ($440K drop in inventory @ 25%)
$325,000 Component inventory carrying cost savings ($1,300K drop in inventory @ 25%)
$435,000 Total benefits expected

Net Savings

$435,000 Total benefits
– $ 10,000 Total cost
$425,000 Expected Savings

Figure 14-4b. Magnum's Cost-Benefit Analysis

COST-BENEFIT ANALYSIS

Team Leader: Bob Smith

Date: February 4, 2009

Team Members: Janet Gains, Paul Johnson, Sam Peterson, Terry Hanson, and Adam Manner

Page **3 of 3**

Estimated Completion:

Expect to meet strategic objective deadline and results.

Comments:

1. Inventory is expected to increase by $800K the first few weeks after implementation as we acquire the proper inventory but will decrease by $435K from current inventory levels within sixteen weeks after implementation.
2. With approval, will proceed.

Figure 14-4c. Magnum's Cost-Benefit Analysis

Step 6: Approval and Secondary Measurements

15

This step involves getting approval to implement and putting secondary measurements in place. The chapter uses the Magnum example to illustrate procedural details.

Getting Approval to Implement

Magnum's controller and the executive sponsor reviewed the BPI team's cost-benefit analysis form and decided that the information was accurate and rational. The team was now ready to present its findings/recommendations to the executive staff for approval. All the material for the presentation was already available; it had been compiled in stages as the team worked through each of the seven administration automation steps.

The progression of steps and the depth of information compiled along the way is exactly what an executive team should expect; the methodology produces a well-researched, well-thought-out solution that includes financial data on costs and benefits. From this comprehensive array of data, the BPI team should create two packets: a main presentation packet and a secondary presentation packet.

As Figure 15-1 illustrates, the main packet consists of the following:

- **Root Cause Analysis Worksheet:** This led the team to identify the affected process.
- **Affected Process Sequence Chart:** This chart provided the visibility of what was occurring.
- **Future Process Sequence Chart:** This chart is the result of questioning the current technique and brainstorming to create a more suitable process for the environment.
- **Implementation Milestone Chart:** This chart represents the step-by-step plan of how the solutions will be implemented and by when.
- **Cost-Benefit Analysis:** This reflects what is required financially to bring about the solution. It also reflects the benefits that should come from implementing the solutions and associated dollar benefits. The analysis reaffirms that the solutions, if adopted, will achieve the strategic objective.

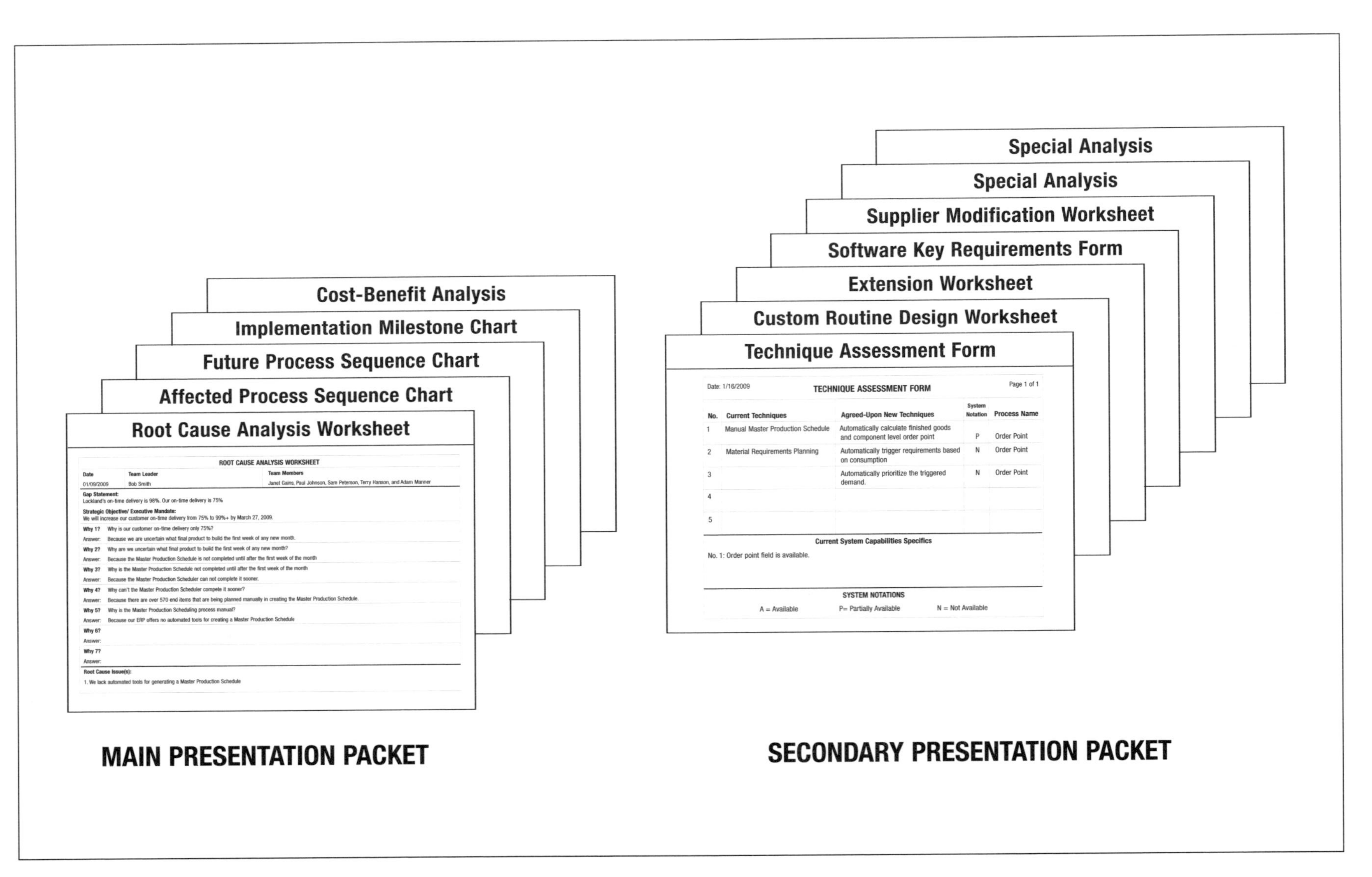

Figure 15-1. Main Presentation Packet and Secondary Presentation Packet

The secondary presentation package contains additional information that may be required if management has additional questions or requests additional details. The secondary packet may include:

- **Technique Assessment Form:** This form reflects the work of the BPI team in determining whether the current package contained the desired capabilities.
- **Custom Routine Design Worksheets (if applied):** This is the document that will be used to program the routine(s). It reflects the step-by-step logic of the program, input screens, output screens and reports, and the status of required data.
- **Extension Worksheets (if applied):** This document is used to 1) attach a routine to an existing hook, or 2) create a copy of the existing module and modify its functionality. This guides the programmer how to put into place the desired enhancement(s).
- **Software Key Requirements Form (if applied):** This form reflects the key requirements sought and the rating for each package that was demonstrated.
- **Supplier Modification Worksheet (if applied):** This document is used to communicate to the supplier the required modifications to the standard package.

Other documents and materials that may have a bearing on findings and recommendations can also be included. For its presentation to management, for example, the Magnum team prepared overhead slides, and the team's secondary presentation packet included three inventory analysis reports that the material manager created when determining inventory projections.

All members of the BPI team should participate in the presentation to the executive team. One team member opens the presentation with a summary of the project and its potential, but all team members may be called on to answer questions posed by the executive staff. At Magnum, it was agreed that the BPI team leader would present the material. The team also planned to keep the answers brief and to avoid technical jargon.

The team's thorough preparation paid off: Magnum management approved the project.

Putting Secondary Measurements in Place

Once approval for a project is secured, it is time to put secondary measurements in place. Secondary measurements are used to monitor the affects of the new techniques being implemented. Suppose, for example, you wanted to improve the on-time picking of merchandise from the warehouse, and the root cause issue of being late was not knowing the projected load hours so that you could staff properly. If you put into place a load versus capacity routine, the primary measurement would be items picked on time. The secondary measurement might be average pick time based on accumulated hours worked versus the number of line items picked (efficiency) to ensure you are not inadvertently overstaffing.

The Magnum BPI team's strategic objective was to increase the customer on-time delivery from 75 percent to 99 percent or better by March 27, 2009. To achieve this, they decided to put in a new order-point system. For its primary measurement (see Chapter 10), the team chose to monitor customer on-time delivery weekly. Prior to implementation, the team discussed and selected the secondary measurements that should be put into place:

- Finish goods inventory levels
- Component inventory levels
- Work-in-process inventory levels
- Component line shortages

All four measurements already existed in some form; however, the new performance charts would have a baseline and anticipated levels of performance by time period. The results would be charted weekly and posted on the BPI team's workroom wall.

Additional Key Point

The overall process of creating a lean office produces the documentation necessary to obtain approval for implementation. It reflects the due diligence that would be expected by any executive team, which speaks to the thoroughness of the techniques that have been demonstrated.

Step 7: Implementation

16

To ensure that the system is implemented correctly, the BPI team must do the following:

- Review, update, and discuss the Implementation Milestone Chart several times a week to ensure that everything is on schedule.
- Attend every BPI meeting and address any concerns. This is a team effort; if someone needs help, find a way of getting that team member assistance.
- Everyone must be available on the day of implementation. Do not wait for the users to approach the team with issues. The BPI team should work with users to ensure the system is working as designed and is being applied correctly.
- Ensure that the users have been trained to handle the exceptions. The single biggest reason systems fail is exceptions.

Monitoring Measurements

Once the system is implemented, it is critical to monitor (routinely and frequently) the primary and secondary measurements to ensure that the expected results are being achieved. Until the strategic objectives are realized, management should be updated on a periodic basis. A one-page status summary with a copy of the measurement charts, which clearly reflects what should occur compared with what is occurring, is an ideal tool for this. The team must immediately investigate any measurement that is not going according to plan and rectify any issues. The team remains intact until the strategic objective(s) are realized.

The Magnum BPI team met a minimum of three times a week during the implementation phase. During this period, custom routines were programmed and tested, procedures were written, and cable was laid to connect to the new terminals. On the day of the implementation, the team went to the workstations of all the users of the system every hour, talking to everyone, answering all questions, and checking to see if the system was operating smoothly. They kept top-level management apprised of the status on a regular basis.

Keeping the Team in Place

After everything was implemented, the BPI team remained in place until the strategic objective was realized. The team monitored the measurements constantly and made slight adjustments to the programs based on user input. The team could tell from the secondary measurement of shortages that the safety stock level for components needed to increase slightly. Because they understood the difference between symptom and root cause, they first investigated to ascertain that the shortage increase was not caused by machine breakdowns, absenteeism, and so on. They found that it was caused by a slight degree of nonlinear demand patterns requiring additional safety stock and made a slight adjustment to the safety stock setting. The overall inventory adjusted, just as predicted. It first climbed upward and then down to the levels expected. The customer on-time delivery rate climbed rapidly and remained at 99 percent or better.

Additional Key Points

- The measurements during and directly after the turn-on date of the enhancements are typically monitored to review daily results. This way, any unexpected shifts in results can be addressed and rectified immediately. The results charted and presented are still typically based upon weekly increments.
- It normally takes a few weeks for everyone to get used to the new techniques and systems. Continue with team presence at the site where the changes are being applied until it is perfectly clear that everyone is totally comfortable with how the system is functioning.

CONCLUSION

The seven steps of administration automation are an exceptional tool for creating the ultimate lean office. There is no limitation to the level of excellence that can be achieved through the application of this methodology. The following list highlights why it is highly effective:

- It is used to create a lean office, regardless if it is being applied to a manufacturing or service-related office.
- It is tied to the strategic objectives of the company.
- It can rectify impediments to satisfying customer expectations or perpetuating the business effectively in terms of speed, accuracy, costs, level of service, and timeliness of completion.
- It can unify disjointed processes.
- It can create a competitive advantage through innovation.
- It eliminates waste and streamlines non-value-addeded activities, leaving only required activities, which are then automated.
- It has its own definition of waste that is commensurate with the capabilities to alleviate it.
- It creates a multiplier effect, freeing staff performing mundane repetitive tasks to performing strategic-level activities.
- It can be applied without changing source code in the vast majority of the cases.
- It can free a company from having to adopt the processes dictated by canned software, which are often incorrect for the environment.
- It creates a communication bridge that replaces the communication gap between IT and the company in defining in detail exactly what is required, even if the gap has existed for years.
- It can create an entire supply chain system that is custom fitted to the specific needs of an entire company or can be applied to an individual, specific issue.
- Last, but certainly not least, is that this methodology was created specifically for the office.

INDEX

ABOUT THE AUTHOR

Raymond S. Louis is founder and CEO of Replenishment Technology Group, Inc., which specializes in supply-chain replenishment systems, lean production, and lean office. He has over thirty years of hands-on experience in assessing, rectifying, designing, and implementing replenishment and lean office systems—internationally—for a multitude of companies, and is recognized as one of the world's leading authorities on designing and implementing highly effective supply-chain systems. He has authored a number of books including: *Integrating Kanban with MRPII* and *Custom Kanban Designing the System to Meet the Needs of Your Environment* (Productivity Press). He has taught at the University of California and California State University. He has worked for major corporations, holding a wide range of professional titles: vice president of corporate logistics, operations manager, manufacturing manager, materials manager, purchasing manager, and inventory control manager. He has an MBA and is certified CPIM by the American Production and Inventory Control Society and CPM by the Institute for Supply Management. Mr. Louis welcomes comments, suggestions, questions, and feedback concerning this work. He can be reached by e-mail at: *kanban@kanban.us*.